Extreme Twisties

D1475984

Southeastern USA

by
William Long

Editor / Cover Design: William Long
Copyright TXu 864-780
ISBN - 0-9671257-0-7

To order additional copies of *Extreme Twisties, Southeastern USA* **($14.95),** you may send your name and shipping address with payment (**plus $2.50** shipping & handling) to:
L & A Publishing
P.O. Box 7158
Chestnut Mtn., GA 30502
*Or place a credit card order through our website at: **http://www.extremetwisties.com**
*Or call us at (770) 535-2537 between the hours of 9:00 am - 5:00 pm M-F

Extreme Twisties combines the best of the best in roads for traveling by sportscar, or motorcycle. I selected these roads for what they will offer you in beauty, challenges, and excitement. In this edition of Extreme Twisties, I have included a selection of roads that run throughout the Southeastern United States. Roads from the States of GA, KY, NC, TN, VA, and WV can be found in this book. I continue to find myself on a never ending search for that ultimate riding experience. Whether I am riding my white knuckles road burner VMax, the ride a rail R1100S, or driving my classic 1982 Alfa Spider, I am constantly on a quest for that thrilling open road experience.

This book actually started as a collection of penciled in references on roads I liked to frequent on my travels in the Southeastern United States. After a while, I found many drawings, maps, notes, and a variety of other references in places ranging from desk drawers to tank bags. It became a little frustrating to remember where I had left the information from last week, last month, or even last year. Too many roads, too much time, or just too bad of a memory. I knew it was time to make some changes. I needed to organize, and use some sort of method to track all of these great roads.

My collection of roads grew greater as the years passed. I decided to make a record, which would allow me to better track the information on each road. Several friends I traveled with encouraged me to make this information available for everyone. I believe they might have been talking about themselves, but I took it to mean I should write this book for folks like yourself. And so the long process of putting Extreme Twisties together began. Choosing the roads became the most difficult task in writing this book. Deciding what roads to include, and which ones to eliminate became quite a chore. I found myself becoming more selective as I drove through the many backroads. I wanted to include only those roads, which would make the traveler long for their next trip.

When classifying a run it is important to consider the degree of riding difficulty one experiences on the road. I have included a variety of runs that range in difficulty; from lazy sweepers, and easy curves, to the roads which will bring one to the edge of destruction, and leave you questioning your chances of surviving another encounter. The concentration, coordination, and skill level required to complete the runs will vary, as will the variety of scenarios, elevations, and sites. The selection is designed to offer you a choice of runs that will help when planning a fantastic road trip. Many of the runs are a collection of great roads linked together to form a loop, or an extended run. These road combinations are perfect for a day of adventurous road travel.

To help you find that special road, or plan a great road trip, I have included the state maps indicating actual run locations, and a detailed road map showing you the entire run. There is a summary on each run listing sites of interest, as well as, a complete road evaluation sheet that will assist you in selecting the right run for that special road trip. The Road Evaluation Sheet includes a wide variety of valuable information on each run. From run distances, elevations, and speed limits, to a complete listing of the type of roads, and curves you will experience are noted on the evaluation sheet. Road hazards are always part of a motoring trip, and should be seriously considered when traveling through the unfamiliar countryside. The road hazards check list will help you to determine the obstacles you might encounter. As road conditions do change, always be on the lookout for the unexpected hazard.

I hope Extreme Twisties will be a helpful travel guide to you, and your friends. Not all the great roads could be included in this first edition of Extreme Twisties - Southeastern United States. My travels take me through many beautiful areas, and along some of the best roads in the country. I will continue to share these experiences in future books. May your road trips be always safe, and full of exciting adventures.

TABLE OF CONTENTS

CODE REFERENCES

ROAD ABBREVIATION:
SR-STATE ROUTE; US-US HIGHWAY

MAP / ROAD LOCATION:
N-NORTH; S-SOUTH; E-EAST; W-WEST; C-CENTRAL

REFERENCE GUIDE
RUN SHEET
State ID
Run Name
State Map Location - Road ID
STATE MAP
Star Shows Run# (R#) Location

GEORGIA
Twisties

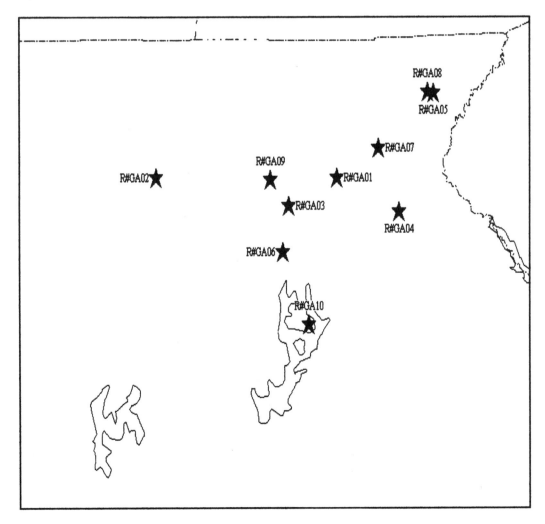

GEORGIA RUN LIST

REFERENCE GUIDE
RUN SHEET
State ID
Run Name
State Map Location - Road ID
STATE MAP
Star Shows Run# (R#) Location

GA
Richard B. Russell Pkwy
NE - SR348

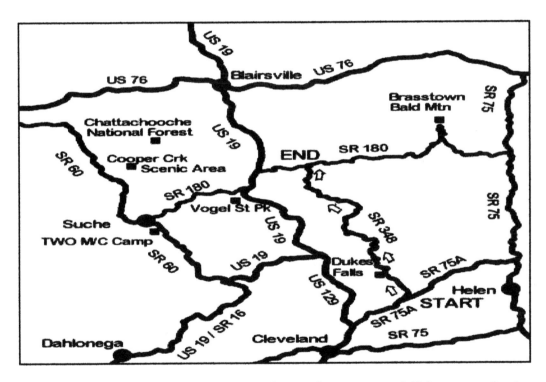

The North Georgia mountains parkway is a great addition to a day's run. The Chattahooche National Forest surrounds you with terrific views, and several hiking areas you are sure to enjoy. Dukes Creek Falls is a relaxing area to take a walk. The panoramic overlooks show the true beauty of the North Georgia mountains. Challenging curves, and fast sweepers make this an exciting ride for everyone.

Road Evaluation

ROAD REFERENCE: R#GA01 - RICHARD B. RUSSELL PARKWAY

RUN DISTANCE: 24- Miles

ELEVATION: 1750- Ft > 3200- Ft

SPEED LIMITS: XXX- 15-25mph   XXX- 35mph   XXX- 45mph   _____55mph   _____65+mph

RUN EVALUATION: _____Lots Of Fun // A Run To Remember

XXX- A Blast To Run // Plenty Of Curves

_____Great Run // Major Challenges

_____Extreme Ride // Surprises At Every Turn

TYPE OF ROAD:

XXX- Sweepers	XXX- Two Lane Traffic
XXX- Flowing Curves	_____Four Lane Traffic
XXX-Tight Curves	XXX- Scenic Overlooks / Views
_____Extreme Curves	XXX- National / State Parks

TYPE OF CURVES: XXX- Right Angles   _____Uies   _____Zs   XXX- Ss

POSSIBLE ROAD HAZARDS:

_____Rain Grooves	XXX- Loose Gravel / Sand	_____Pot Holes
XXX- Slick Tar Spots	_____Tunnels	_____Narrow Road
_____Bad Banking Curves	_____Un-Even Pavement	_____Animal Xings
XXX- Pedestrians	XXX- Rd Shoulder Drop-Offs	XXX- Blind Curves
XXX- Water Run-Offs	_____Pavement Cracking	XXX- Rock Fall Areas

OVER ALL ROAD CONDITIONS: _____Ok   _____Good   _____Great   XXX- Exc

GA
Fort Mountain
NC - SR2

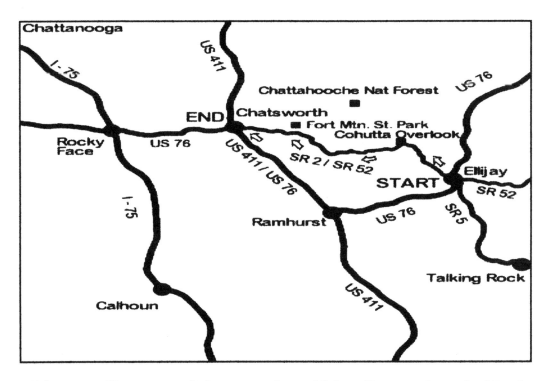

This run offers one of the most beautiful valley settings in North Georgia. Follow the Mountaintown Creek as it flows through a valley surrounded by rolling hills. Some places of interest are the Cohutta overlook in the Chattahooche National Forest, or the Fort Mountain State Park. Cabin rentals at Fort Mountain provide you with a great stop-over. This is an easy run with long sweepers and twisting curves.

Road Evaluation

ROAD REFERENCE: R#GA02 - FORT MOUNTAIN

RUN DISTANCE: 27- Miles

ELEVATION: 900- Ft > 3400- Ft

SPEED LIMITS: XXX- 15-25mph XXX- 35mph XXX- 45mph _____55mph _____65+mph

RUN EVALUATION: _____Lots Of Fun // A Run To Remember

                        XXX- A Blast To Run // Plenty Of Curves

                        _____Great Run // Major Challenges

                        _____Extreme Ride // Surprises At Every Turn

TYPE OF ROAD: XXX- Sweepers   XXX- Two Lane Traffic

                        XXX- Flowing Curves   _____Four Lane Traffic

                        XXX- Tight Curves   XXX- Scenic Overlooks / Views

                        _____Extreme Curves   XXX- National / State Parks

TYPE OF CURVES: _____Right Angles _____Uies _____Zs XXX- Ss

POSSIBLE ROAD
HAZARDS: _____Rain Grooves   XXX- Loose Gravel / Sand   _____Pot Holes

                        XXX- Slick Tar Spots   _____Tunnels   XXX- Narrow Road

                        _____Bad Banking Curves _____Un-Even Pavement   XXX- Animal Xings

                        XXX- Pedestrians   XXX- Rd Shoulder Drop-Offs   _____Blind Curves

                        XXX- Water Run-Offs   XXX- Pavement Cracking   _____Rock Fall Areas

OVER ALL ROAD
CONDITIONS: _____Ok XXX- Good _____Great _____Exc

GA
Toccoa River
NC - SR60

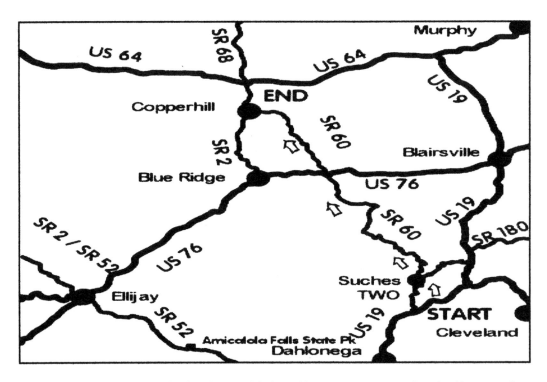

Enjoy a ride through the beautiful valley curves, and challenge the ruggedness of the Chattahoochee National Forest. The Chestatee overlook provides you a great view of this area. For trout fishing try the Toccoa River, or Cooper Creek. Two-Wheels-Only, located in Suches, is a great M/C campground. Comfortable lodging is available. This run is highlighted by a variety of great curves, and sweepers. Enjoy!!!

Road Evaluation

ROAD REFERENCE: **R#GA03 - TOCCOA RIVER**

RUN DISTANCE: 48- Miles

ELEVATION: 1500- Ft > 3000- Ft

SPEED LIMITS: XXX- 15-25mph XXX- 35mph XXX- 45mph XXX- 55mph _____65+mph

RUN EVALUATION:

_____Lots Of Fun // A Run To Remember

_____A Blast To Run // Plenty Of Curves

XXX- Great Run // Major Challenges

_____Extreme Ride // Surprises At Every Turn

TYPE OF ROAD:

XXX- Sweepers	XXX- Two Lane Traffic
XXX- Flowing Curves	_____Four Lane Traffic
XXX- Tight Curves	XXX- Scenic Overlooks / Views
XXX- Extreme Curves	XXX- National / State Parks

TYPE OF CURVES: XXX- Right Angles   XXX- Uies   XXX- Zs   XXX- Ss

POSSIBLE ROAD HAZARDS:

_____Rain Grooves	XXX- Loose Gravel / Sand	XXX- Pot Holes
XXX- Slick Tar Spots	_____Tunnels	XXX- Narrow Road
XXX- Bad Banking Curves	XXX- Un-Even Pavement	XXX- Animal Xings
_____Pedestrians	XXX- Rd Shoulder Drop-Offs	XXX- Blind Curves
XXX- Water Run-Offs	XXX- Pavement Cracking	_____Rock Fall Areas

OVER ALL ROAD CONDITIONS: _____Ok   XXX- Good   _____Great   _____Exc

GA
Falls Mountain
NE - SR197

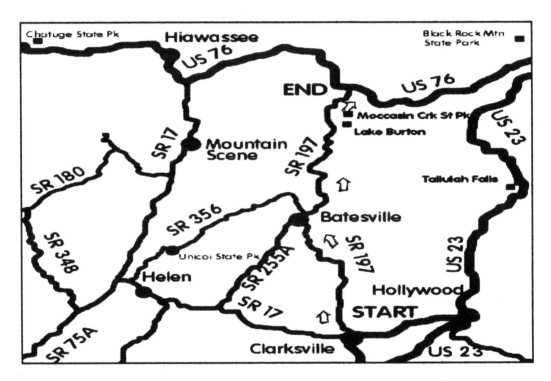

There are some great spots to check out along this run. The southern charm, and good meals at the Batesville General Store are good for all. The mountain stream, and waterfall at Grandpa Watts pottery shop is a perfect pull-over for everyone. Stop by Lake Burton's Fish Hatchery, or camp out at the Moccasin Creek State Park. For the best twisties, try the Lake Burton area. Challenging curves, but not overpowering.

Road Evaluation

ROAD REFERENCE: **R#GA04 - FALLS MOUNTAIN**

RUN DISTANCE: 26- Miles

ELEVATION: 1350- Ft > 2300- Ft

SPEED LIMITS: _____15-25mph XXX- 35mph XXX- 45mph _____55mph _____65+mph

RUN EVALUATION: _____Lots Of Fun // A Run To Remember

XXX- A Blast To Run // Plenty Of Curves

_____Great Run // Major Challenges

_____Extreme Ride // Surprises At Every Turn

TYPE OF ROAD:

XXX- Sweepers	XXX- Two Lane Traffic
XXX- Flowing Curves	_____Four Lane Traffic
XXX- Tight Curves	XXX- Scenic Overlooks / Views
_____Extreme Curves	XXX- National / State Parks

TYPE OF CURVES: XXX- Right Angles _____Uies _____Zs XXX- Ss

POSSIBLE ROAD HAZARDS:

_____Rain Grooves	XXX- Loose Gravel / Sand	XXX- Pot Holes
XXX- Slick Tar Spots	_____Tunnels	XXX- Narrow Road
_____Bad Banking Curves	XXX- Un-Even Pavement	XXX- Animal Xings
_____Pedestrians	_____Rd Shoulder Drop-Offs	XXX- Blind Curves
_____Water Run-Offs	XXX- Pavement Cracking	_____Rock Fall Areas

OVER ALL ROAD CONDITIONS: _____Ok XXX- Good _____Great _____Exc

GA - NC
War Woman Loop
NE-WarWoman/Sr28/106/US23

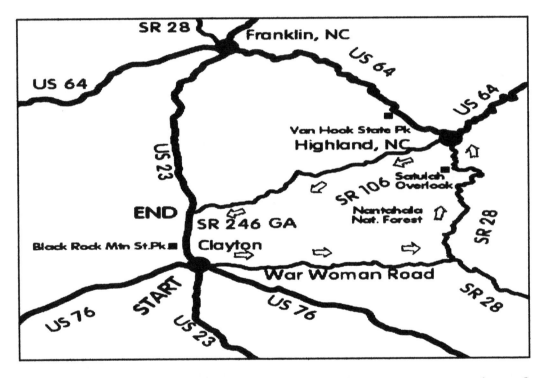

This run offers it all, from valley runs to the extreme cornering of mountain roads. You will wind through the curves of the Nantahala National Forest, see a waterfall at the Satulah Overlook, and shop in the quaint town of Highland, NC. This loop will take you from GA to NC and back again. You'll run everything from open valley sweepers to the narrow mountain twisties. Riding with caution is a must! Have Fun!!!

Road Evaluation

ROAD REFERENCE: R#GA05 - WAR WOMAN LOOP

RUN DISTANCE: 50- Miles

ELEVATION: 1650- Ft > 4150- Ft

SPEED LIMITS: XXX- 15-25mph XXX- 35mph XXX- 45mph XXX- 55mph _____65+mph

RUN EVALUATION: _____Lots Of Fun // A Run To Remember

                           _____A Blast To Run // Plenty Of Curves

                           XXX- Great Run // Major Challenges

                           _____Extreme Ride // Surprises At Every Turn

TYPE OF ROAD: _____Sweepers   XXX- Two Lane Traffic

                           XXX- Flowing Curves   XXX- Four Lane Traffic

                           XXX- Tight Curves   XXX- Scenic Overlooks / Views

                           XXX- Extreme Curves   XXX- National / State Parks

TYPE OF CURVES: XXX- Right Angles   XXX- Uies   XXX- Zs   XXX- Ss

POSSIBLE ROAD HAZARDS:

_____Rain Grooves	XXX- Loose Gravel / Sand	_____Pot Holes
_____Slick Tar Spots	_____ Tunnels	XXX- Narrow Road
XXX- Bad Banking Curves	XXX- Un-Even Pavement	_____Animal Xings
_____Pedestrians	XXX- Rd Shoulder Drop-Offs	XXX- Blind Curves
XXX- Water Run-Offs	_____Pavement Cracking	XXX- Rock Fall Areas

OVER ALL ROAD CONDITIONS: _____Ok _____Good   XXX- Great _____Exc

GA
Long Ridge
NC - US19

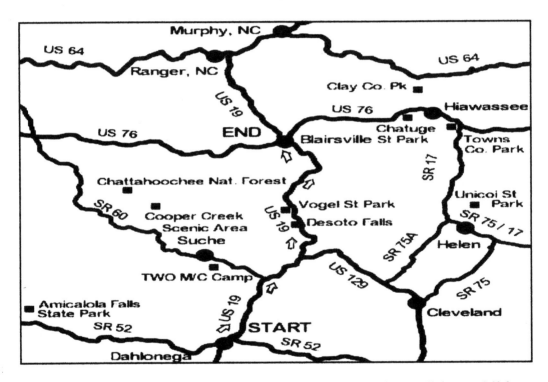

Don't miss this run! Great views, excellent road conditions, hiking trails, and State Parks all add up to make this a great run. The Appalachian Trail at the Walasi-yi Center in the Chattahoochee National Forest is a nice stop to shop, and take in the view. You can enjoy trout fishing, camping, and recreation at Desoto Falls, and Vogel State Park. The low gear curves on this run will keep you pushing those RPMs.

Road Evaluation

ROAD REFERENCE: **R#GA06 - LONG RIDGE**

RUN DISTANCE: 37- Miles

ELEVATION: 1250- Ft > 4500- Ft

SPEED LIMITS: XXX- 15-25mph XXX- 35mph XXX- 45mph XXX- 55mph _____65+mph

RUN EVALUATION: _____Lots Of Fun // A Run To Remember

          _____A Blast To Run // Plenty Of Curves

          XXX- Great Run // Major Challenges

          _____Extreme Ride // Surprises At Every Turn

TYPE OF ROAD:

XXX- Sweepers	XXX- Two Lane Traffic
XXX- Flowing Curves	XXX- Four Lane Traffic
XXX- Tight Curves	XXX- Scenic Overlooks / Views
XXX- Extreme Curves	XXX- National / State Parks

TYPE OF CURVES: XXX- Right Angles XXX- Uies XXX- Zs XXX- Ss

POSSIBLE ROAD HAZARDS:

_____Rain Grooves	XXX- Loose Gravel / Sand	_____Pot Holes
XXX- Slick Tar Spots	_____Tunnels	_____Narrow Road
_____Bad Banking Curves	_____Un-Even Pavement	_____Animal Xings
XXX- Pedestrians	XXX- Rd Shoulder Drop-Offs	XXX- Blind Curves
XXX- Water Run-Offs	_____Pavement Cracking	XXX- Rock Fall Areas

OVER ALL ROAD CONDITIONS: _____Ok _____Good _____Great XXX- Exc

GA
Brasstown Bald Mtn
NE - SR356/75/180/SR180Spur

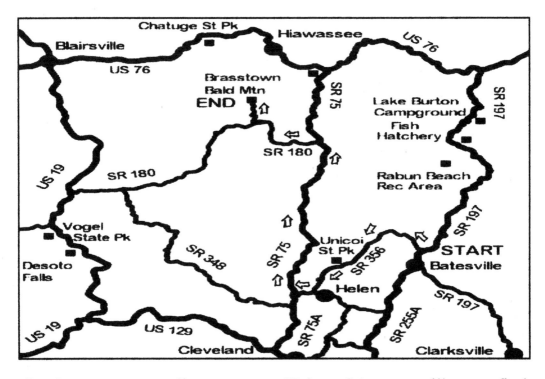

Starting out as a valley run near Helen, GA, you will soon find yourself travelling along the Chattahoochee River, by the Unicoi Gap, and through the Unicoi State Park. The final three miles of this run up to the top of Brasstown Bald Mountain are excellent twisties. Smooth, tight curves that are surrounded by fantastic mountain views. A visit to the Brasstown Bald Mountain observertory will cap off a terrific run.

Road Evaluation

ROAD REFERENCE: R#GA07 - BRASSTOWN BALD MOUNTAIN

RUN DISTANCE: 30- Miles

ELEVATION: 1450- Ft > 4250- Ft

SPEED LIMITS: XXX- 15-25mph XXX- 35mph XXX- 45mph XXX- 55mph _____65+mph

RUN EVALUATION:

_____Lots Of Fun // A Run To Remember

XXX- A Blast To Run // Plenty Of Curves

_____Great Run // Major Challenges

_____Extreme Ride // Surprises At Every Turn

TYPE OF ROAD:

XXX- Sweepers	XXX- Two Lane Traffic
XXX- Flowing Curves	XXX- Four Lane Traffic
XXX- Tight Curves	XXX- Scenic Overlooks / Views
_____Extreme Curves	XXX- National / State Parks

TYPE OF CURVES: XXX- Right Angles   XXX- Uies   XXX- Zs   XXX- Ss

POSSIBLE ROAD HAZARDS:

_____Rain Grooves	XXX- Loose Gravel / Sand	_____Pot Holes
XXX- Slick Tar Spots	_____Tunnels	XXX- Narrow Road
_____Bad Banking Curves	_____Un-Even Pavement	_____Animal Xings
XXX- Pedestrians	XXX- Rd Shoulder Drop-Offs	XXX- Blind Curves
_____Water Run-Offs	_____Pavement Cracking	_____Rock Fall Areas

OVER ALL ROAD CONDITIONS: _____Ok _____Good _____Great XXX- Exc

GA
Turkey Gap
NE/NC - US76

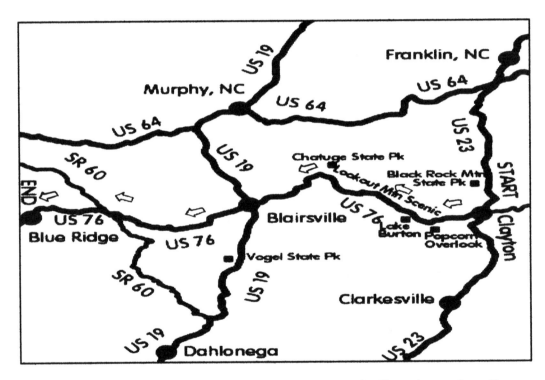

This is a long run with great road conditions winding through valleys, and rolling hills. There are beautiful views of several lake areas you might want to pull over to enjoy. Jones Bridge at Lake Burton, and the Popcorn Overlook, add to an already enjoyable ride in the North Georgia mountains. The high speed sweepers highlight this run, but you will experience several exciting surprises in the corners.

Road Evaluation

ROAD REFERENCE: **R#GA08 - TURKEY GAP**

RUN DISTANCE: 70- Miles

ELEVATION: 1700- Ft > 2700- Ft

SPEED LIMITS: XXX- 15-25mph XXX- 35mph XXX- 45mph XXX- 55mph XXX- 65+mph

RUN EVALUATION: XXX- Lots Of Fun // A Run To Remember

_____A Blast To Run // Plenty Of Curves

_____Great Run // Major Challenges

_____Extreme Ride // Surprises At Every Turn

TYPE OF ROAD:

XXX- Sweepers	XXX- Two Lane Traffic
XXX- Flowing Curves	XXX- Four Lane Traffic
XXX- Tight Curves	XXX- Scenic Overlooks / Views
_____Extreme Curves	XXX- National / State Parks

TYPE OF CURVES: XXX- Right Angles _____Uies _____Zs XXX- Ss

POSSIBLE ROAD HAZARDS:

_____Rain Grooves	_____Loose Gravel / Sand	_____Pot Holes
XXX- Slick Tar Spots	_____Tunnels	_____Narrow Road
_____Bad Banking Curves	_____Un-Even Pavement	_____Animal Xings
XXX- Pedestrians	_____Rd Shoulder Drop-Offs	_____Blind Curves
_____Water Run-Offs	_____Pavement Cracking	_____Rock Fall Areas

OVER ALL ROAD CONDITIONS: _____Ok _____Good _____Great XXX- Exc

GA
Wolf Pen / Panther Gap
NC - SR180

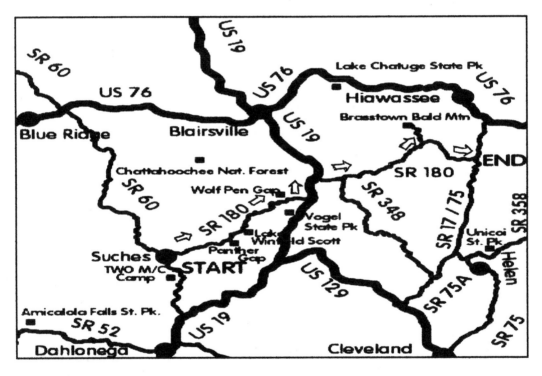

Lake Winfield Scott, Vogel State Park, and Brasstown Bald Mountain are some of the great high points on this run. Extreme curves, narrow roads, and blind curves combined to make this run one of the most exciting, and lethal runs in GA. Many dare devils have met their demise on the sharp curves of SR180. Extreme caution should be taken on the section running between Vogel State Park and Suches at SR60. The curves leave you little room for making errors.

Road Evaluation

ROAD REFERENCE: **R#GA09 - WOLF PEN / PANTHER GAP**

RUN DISTANCE: 30- Miles

ELEVATION: 1900- Ft > 3750- Ft

SPEED LIMITS: XXX- 15-25mph XXX- 35mph XXX- 45mph XXX- 55mph _____65+mph

RUN EVALUATION: _____Lots Of Fun // A Run To Remember

_____A Blast To Run // Plenty of Curves

_____Great Run // Major Challenges

XXX- Extreme Ride // Surprises at Every Turn

TYPE OF ROAD:

XXX- Sweepers	XXX- Two Lane Traffic
XXX- Flowing Curves	_____Four Lane Traffic
XXX- Tight Curves	XXX- Scenic Overlooks / Views
XXX- Extreme Curves	XXX- National / State Parks

TYPE OF CURVES: XXX- Right Angles XXX- Uies XXX- Zs XXX- Ss

POSSIBLE ROAD HAZARDS:

_____Rain Grooves	XXX- Loose Gravel / Sand	XXX- Pot Holes
XXX- Slick Tar Spots	_____Tunnels	XXX- Narrow Road
_____Bad Banking Curves	XXX- Un-Even Pavement	XXX- Animal Xings
XXX- Pedestrians	XXX- Rd Shoulder Drop-Offs	XXX- Blind Curves
XXX- Water Run-Offs	XXX- Pavement Cracking	XXX- Rock Fall Areas

OVER ALL ROAD CONDITIONS: _____ Ok XXX- Good _____Great _____Exc

GA
Carters Lake
NC - SR136

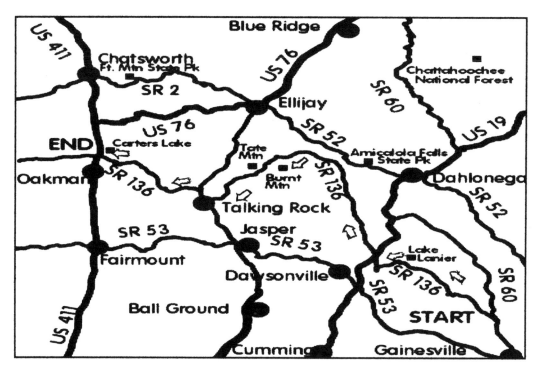

From the scenic views of Lake Lanier to the panoramic overlooks at Tate and Burnt Mountain, this run makes for a great day. Carters Lake offers a nice place for an afternoon adventure of hiking, fishing, or just laying back. The camping facilities are nice for a comfortable overnight stop. Flowing sweepers through the North GA pasture lands, and mountain tops highlight this run. Smooth running!

Road Evaluation

ROAD REFERENCE: R#GA10 - CARTER'S LAKE

RUN DISTANCE: 58- Miles

ELEVATION: 750- Ft > 3150- Ft

SPEED LIMITS: XXX- 15-25mph XXX- 35mph XXX- 45mph XXX- 55mph _____65+mph

RUN EVALUATION:
- _____ Lots Of Fun // A Run To Remember
- XXX- A Blast To Run // Plenty Of Curves
- _____Great Run // Major Challenges
- _____Extreme Ride // Surprises At Every Turn

TYPE OF ROAD:

XXX- Sweepers	XXX- Two Lane Traffic
XXX- Flowing Curves	XXX- Four Lane Traffic
XXX- Tight Curves	XXX- Scenic Overlooks / Views
_____Extreme Curves	XXX- National / State Parks

TYPE OF CURVES: XXX- Right Angles _____Uies _____Zs XXX- Ss

POSSIBLE ROAD HAZARDS:

_____Rain Grooves	XXX- Loose Gravel / Sand	_____Pot Holes
_____Slick Tar Spots	_____Tunnels	_____Narrow Road
_____Bad Banking Curves	XXX- Un-Even Pavement	_____Animal Xings
XXX- Pedestrians	XXX- Rd Shoulder Drop-Offs	_____Blind Curves
XXX- Water Run-Offs	XXX- Pavement Cracking	XXX- Rock Fall Areas

OVER ALL ROAD CONDITIONS: _____Ok _____Good XXX- Great _____Exc

KENTUCKY
Twisties

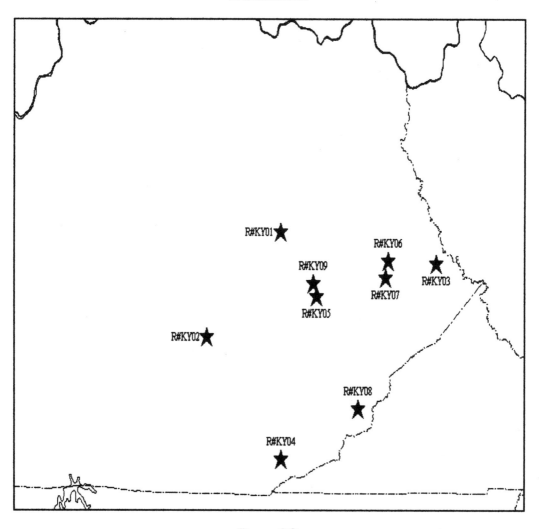

KENTUCKY RUN LIST

REFERENCE GUIDE
RUN SHEET
State ID
Run Name
State Map Location - Road ID
STATE MAP
Star Shows Run# (R#) Location

KY
Red River
EC - SR715/SR77

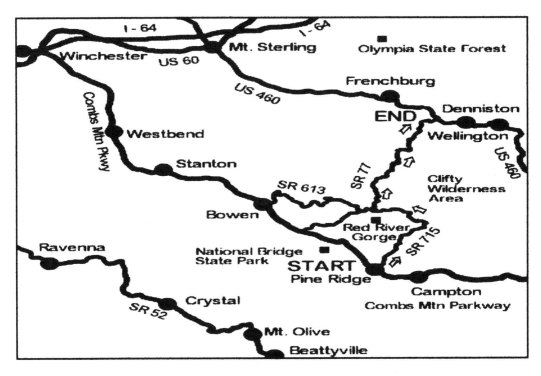

This run is the best in Kentucky backroad experiences. Your travels will take you through the beautiful Red River Gorge Geological Area. The region is called the Clifty Wilderness, and is part of the Daniel Boone National Forest. This forest area is covered with great hiking trails, fishing spots, and picnic areas. A series of fine dip and twist curves will continually challenge you on this narrow forest road.

Road Evaluation

ROAD REFERENCE: **R#KY01 - RED RIVER**

RUN DISTANCE: 28- Miles

ELEVATION: 700- Ft > 1450- Ft

SPEED LIMITS: XXX- 15-25mph XXX- 35mph XXX- 45mph _____55mph _____65+mph

RUN EVALUATION: _____Lots Of Fun // A Run To Remember

XXX- A Blast To Run // Plenty Of Curves

_____Great Run // Major Challenges

_____Extreme Ride // Surprises At Every Turn

TYPE OF ROAD:
XXX- Sweepers	XXX- Two Lane Traffic
XXX- Flowing Curves	_____Four Lane Traffic
XXX- Tight Curves	_____Scenic Overlooks / Views
_____Extreme Curves	XXX- National / State Parks

TYPE OF CURVES: XXX- Right Angles   XXX- Uies   _____Zs   XXX- Ss

POSSIBLE ROAD HAZARDS:
_____Rain Grooves	XXX- Loose Gravel / Sand	XXX- Pot Holes
_____Slick Tar Spots	_____Tunnels	XXX- Narrow Road
_____Bad Banking Curves	XXX- Un-Even Pavement	XXX- Animal Xings
_____Pedestrians	XXX- Rd Shoulder Drop-Offs	XXX- Blind Curves
XXX- Water Run-Offs	XXX- Pavement Cracking	XXX- Rock Fall Areas

OVER ALL ROAD CONDITIONS: _____Ok   _____Good   XXX- Great   _____Exc

KY
Lawson Hollow
SC - SR490/SR89/SR52

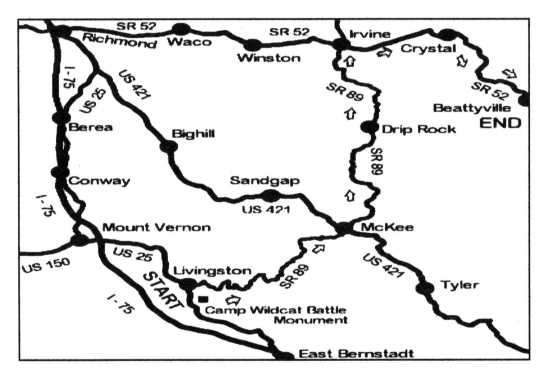

The Kentucky Scenic Byway is a nature trail for vehicles. Following along the Rockcastle River, surrounded by the beautiful countryside, you'll appreciate the simpler side of life. For that special spot to pass the afternoon, you might try the Turkey Foot Recreational Area. Great sweepers, and tight curves provide some major thrills on this run. The ridges offer you the best in valley views, and exciting curves.

Road Evaluation

ROAD REFERENCE: **R#KY02 - LAWSON HOLLOW**

RUN DISTANCE: 85- Miles

ELEVATION: 700- Ft > 1450- Ft

SPEED LIMITS: XXX- 15-25mph XXX- 35mph XXX- 45mph XXX- 55mph _____65+mph

RUN EVALUATION: _____Lots Of Fun // A Run To Remember

XXX- A Blast To Run // Plenty Of Curves

_____Great Run // Major Challenges

_____Extreme Ride // Surprises At Every Turn

TYPE OF ROAD:

XXX- Sweepers	XXX- Two Lane Traffic
XXX- Flowing Curves	_____Four Lane Traffic
XXX- Tight Curves	XXX- Scenic Overlooks / Views
XXX- Extreme Curves	XXX- National / State Parks

TYPE OF CURVES: XXX- Right Angles XXX- Uies XXX- Zs XXX- Ss

POSSIBLE ROAD HAZARDS:

_____Rain Grooves	XXX- Loose Gravel / Sand	XXX- Pot Holes
XXX- Slick Tar Spots	_____Tunnels	XXX- Narrow Road
_____Bad Banking Curves	XXX- Un-Even Pavement	XXX- Animal Xings
_____Pedestrians	XXX- Rd Shoulder Drop-Offs	XXX- Blind Curves
XXX- Water Run-Offs	XXX- Pavement Cracking	XXX- Rock Fall Areas

OVER ALL ROAD CONDITIONS: _____Ok XXX- Good _____Great _____Exc

KY
Tug Fork River
EC - SR468/SR292

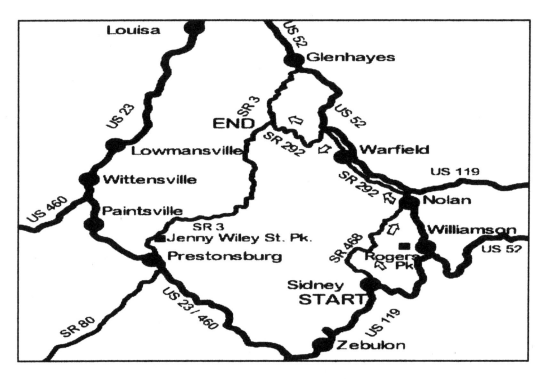

Moving through the Kentucky coal mining countryside, you'll appreciate the life style of the rural communities. Enjoying the serenity of the Tug Fork River flowing beside the road is equally rewarding. Lay back, and relax at one of the many river pull off areas. You'll find this twistie forest / river run is both beautiful, and challenging to ride. The tight "S" curves are well placed between the sweepers. Careful!

Road Evaluation

ROAD REFERENCE: **R#KY03 - TUG FORK RIVER**

RUN DISTANCE: 54- Miles

ELEVATION: 600- Ft > 1250- Ft

SPEED LIMITS: XXX- 15-25mph XXX- 35mph XXX- 45mph _____55mph   _____65+mph

RUN EVALUATION: _____Lots Of Fun // A Run To Remember

XXX- A Blast To Run // Plenty Of Curves

_____Great Run // Major Challenges

_____Extreme Ride // Surprises At Every Turn

TYPE OF ROAD:

XXX- Sweepers	XXX- Two Lane Traffic
XXX- Flowing Curves	_____Four Lane Traffic
XXX- Tight Curves	_____Scenic Overlooks / Views
_____Extreme Curves	_____National / State Parks

TYPE OF CURVES: XXX- Right Angles _____Uies _____Zs XXX- Ss

POSSIBLE ROAD HAZARDS:

_____Rain Grooves	XXX- Loose Gravel / Sand	_____Pot Holes
_____Slick Tar Spots	_____Tunnels	XXX- Narrow Road
_____Bad Banking Curves	_____Un-Even Pavement	_____Animal Xings
_____Pedestrians	XXX- Rd Shoulder Drop-Offs	XXX- Blind Curves
XXX- Water Run-Offs	XXX- Pavement Cracking	XXX- Rock Fall Areas

OVER ALL ROAD CONDITIONS: _____Ok XXX- Good _____Great _____Exc

KY
Brownies Creek
SE - SR987

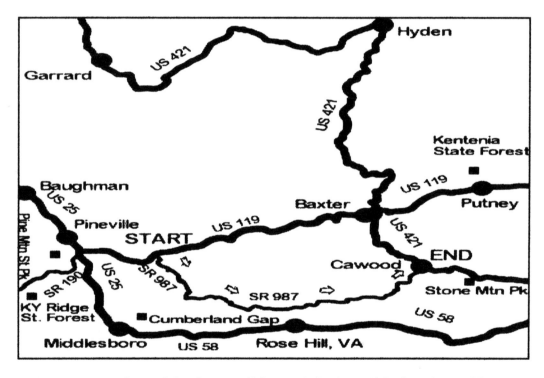

Start your engines, it's time to Dip and Twist. This is a beautiful run that combines open meadows, deep valleys, and thick forests. The Martins Fork Cumberland River, and Brownies Creek wind along this road, adding a special warmth to the ride. The view of the mountains bordering Martins Fork Lake is fantastic. The lake area has several fine recreational facilities to enjoy. Superb wide sweepers highlight this run.

Road Evaluation

ROAD REFERENCE: R#KY04 - BROWNIES CREEK

RUN DISTANCE: 34- Miles

ELEVATION: 1150- Ft > 2500- Ft

SPEED LIMITS: XXX- 15-25mph XXX- 35mph XXX- 45mph _____55mph _____65+mph

RUN EVALUATION:
- _____Lots Of Fun // A Run To Remember
- XXX- A Blast To Run // Plenty Of Curves
- _____Great Run // Major Challenges
- _____Extreme Ride // Surprises At Every Turn

TYPE OF ROAD:

XXX- Sweepers	XXX- Two Lane Traffic
XXX- Flowing Curves	_____Four Lane Traffic
XXX- Tight Curves	XXX- Scenic Overlooks / Views
_____Extreme Curves	_____National / State Parks

TYPE OF CURVES: XXX- Right Angles _____Uies _____Zs XXX- Ss

POSSIBLE ROAD HAZARDS:

_____Rain Grooves	XXX- Loose Gravel / Sand	XXX- Pot Holes
XXX- Slick Tar Spots	XXX- Tunnels	XXX- Narrow Road
XXX- Bad Banking Curves	XXX- Un-Even Pavement	_____Animal Xings
_____Pedestrians	_____Rd Shoulder Drop-Offs	XXX- Blind Curves
XXX- Water Run-Offs	XXX- Pavement Cracking	XXX- Rock Fall Areas

OVER ALL ROAD CONDITIONS: _____Ok XXX- Good _____Great _____Exc

KY
Cat Hollow
EC - SR476/SR550

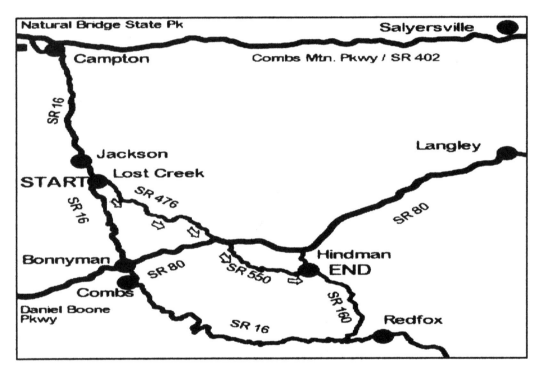

Have fun travelling this scenic valley run as you twist your way down the backroad curves. If suspension bridges are something you look for on a ride, you won't be disappointed. There are over a dozen bridges built across the Troublesome Creek. In the forest areas of SR550, the trees will give you a shaded umbrella effect that is majestic. Tight curves to wide sweepers, combine to make this run special.

Road Evaluation

ROAD REFERENCE: R#KY05 - CAT HOLLOW

RUN DISTANCE: 39- Miles

ELEVATION: 800- Ft > 1350- Ft

SPEED LIMITS: XXX- 15-25mph   XXX- 35mph   XXX- 45mph   _____55mph   _____65+mph

RUN EVALUATION: _____Lots Of Fun // A Run To Remember

XXX- A Blast To Run // Plenty Of Curves

_____Great Run // Major Challenges

_____Extreme Ride // Surprises At Every Turn

TYPE OF ROAD:

XXX- Sweepers	XXX- Two Lane Traffic
XXX- Flowing Curves	_____Four Lane Traffic
XXX- Tight Curves	_____Scenic Overlooks / Views
_____Extreme Curves	_____National / State Parks

TYPE OF CURVES: XXX- Right Angles   XXX- Uies   _____Zs   XXX- Ss

POSSIBLE ROAD HAZARDS:

_____Rain Grooves	XXX- Loose Gravel / Sand	_____Pot Holes
XXX- Slick Tar Spots	_____Tunnels	_____Narrow Road
_____Bad Banking Curves	XXX- Un-Even Pavement	_____Animal Xings
XXX- Pedestrians	XXX- Rd Shoulder Drop-Offs	XXX- Blind Curves
XXX- Water Run-Offs	XXX- Pavement Cracking	XXX- Rock Fall Areas

OVER ALL ROAD CONDITIONS: _____Ok   _____Good   XXX- Great   _____Exc

KY
Rockcastle Creek
EC - SR3

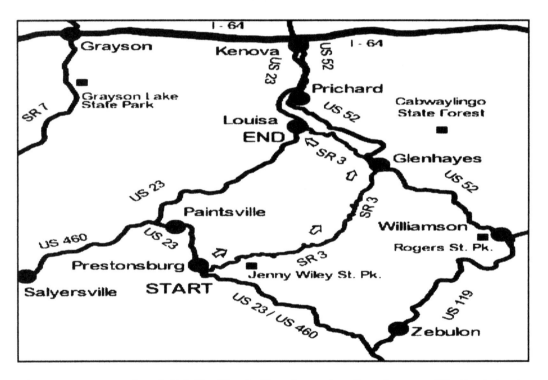

As you cross the Middle Fork Rockcastle Creek, you'll find lush valleys with open fields, surrounded by thick green forests. Just past Inez, the road turns into a four lane highway. The road is a beautiful passage, cutting through the Kentucky mountains. Road conditions are great, as well as, the mountain views. The flowing curves, and high speed sweepers are pure delight. Here is a ride you will surely enjoy.

Road Evaluation

ROAD REFERENCE: R#KY06 - ROCK CASTLE CREEK

RUN DISTANCE: 55- Miles

ELEVATION: 600- Ft > 1200- Ft

SPEED LIMITS: XXX- 15-25mph XXX- 35mph XXX- 45mph XXX- 55mph _____65+mph

RUN EVALUATION:

    _____Lots Of Fun // A Run To Remember

    XXX- A Blast To Run // Plenty Of Curves

    _____Great Run // Major Challenges

    _____Extreme Ride // Surprises At Every Turn

TYPE OF ROAD:

XXX- Sweepers	XXX- Two Lane Traffic
XXX- Flowing Curves	XXX- Four Lane Traffic
XXX- Tight Curves	XXX- Scenic Overlooks / Views
_____Extreme Curves	XXX- National / State Parks

TYPE OF CURVES: XXX- Right Angles _____Uies _____Zs XXX- Ss

POSSIBLE ROAD HAZARDS:

_____Rain Grooves	XXX-Loose Gravel / Sand	XXX- Pot Holes
_____Slick Tar Spots	_____Tunnels	_____Narrow Road
_____Bad Banking Curves	_____Un-Even Pavement	XXX- Animal Xings
_____Pedestrians	XXX- Rd Shoulder Drop-Offs	_____Blind Curves
XXX- Water Run-Offs	XXX- Pavement Cracking	XXX- Rock Fall Areas

OVER ALL ROAD CONDITIONS: _____Ok _____Good XXX- Great _____Exc

KY
Hi Hat
EC - SR122

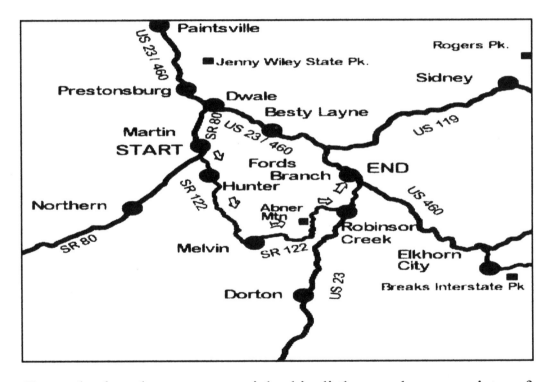

For a backroad country special, this little run has a variety of surroundings that are sure to make your day. From the valleys to the mountains, you will marvel at the warm, and subtle nature of this region. Pulling off next to the Left Fork Beaver Creek, I had a chance to enjoy the area. The blend of lazy sweepers in the valley, and tight curves winding around Abner Mountain, all add to the thrill of this great ride.

Road Evaluation

ROAD REFERENCE: R#KY07 - HI HAT

RUN DISTANCE: 43- Miles

ELEVATION: 700- Ft > 1700- Ft

SPEED LIMITS: XXX- 15-25mph XXX- 35mph XXX- 45mph XXX- 55mph _____65+mph

RUN EVALUATION: _____Lots Of Fun // A Run To Remember

_____A Blast To Run // Plenty Of Curves

XXX- Great Run // Major Challenges

_____Extreme Ride // Surprises At Every Turn

TYPE OF ROAD:

XXX- Sweepers	XXX- Two Lane Traffic
XXX- Flowing Curves	_____Four Lane Traffic
XXX- Tight Curves	_____Scenic Overlooks / Views
_____Extreme Curves	_____National / State Parks

TYPE OF CURVES: XXX- Right Angles   XXX- Uies   _____Zs   XXX- Ss

POSSIBLE ROAD HAZARDS:

_____Rain Grooves	XXX- Loose Gravel / Sand	_____Pot Holes
_____Slick Tar Spots	_____Tunnels	_____Narrow Road
_____Bad Banking Curves	XXX- Un-Even Pavement	XXX- Animal Xings
XXX- Pedestrians	XXX- Rd Shoulder Drop-Offs	XXX- Blind Curves
_____Water Run-Offs	_____Pavement Cracking	XXX- Rock Fall Areas

OVER ALL ROAD CONDITIONS: _____Ok _____Good XXX- Great _____Exc

KY
Oven Fork
EC - US119

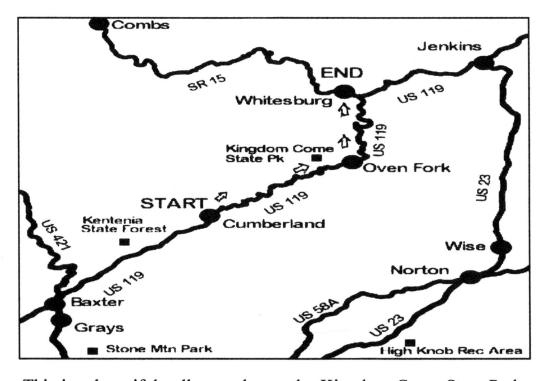

This is a beautiful valley road near the Kingdom Come State Park. The run offers you the enjoyment of riding along the Poor Fork Cumberland River. You will soon find yourself in the Kentucky hills experiencing the winding curves of the Wildlife Management Areas. Super valley sweepers accompany you to the ridges leading up to Whitesburg, KY. There you will enjoy some sharp cornering that will test the best.

Road Evaluation

ROAD REFERENCE: **R#KY08 - OVEN FORK**

RUN DISTANCE: 26- Miles

ELEVATION: 1200- Ft > 2500- Ft

SPEED LIMITS: XXX- 15-25mph XXX- 35mph XXX- 45mph XXX- 55mph _____65+mph

RUN EVALUATION: _____Lots Of Fun // A Run To Remember

XXX- A Blast To Run // Plenty Of Curves

_____Great Run // Major Challenges

_____Extreme Ride // Surprises At Every Turn

TYPE OF ROAD: XXX- Sweepers   XXX- Two Lane Traffic

XXX- Flowing Curves   XXX- Four Lane Traffic

XXX- Tight Curves   XXX- Scenic Overlooks / Views

XXX- Extreme Curves   XXX- National / State Parks

TYPE OF CURVES: XXX- Right Angles   XXX- Uies   XXX- Zs   XXX- Ss

POSSIBLE ROAD HAZARDS:

_____Rain Grooves   XXX- Loose Gravel / Sand   _____Pot Holes

_____Slick Tar Spots   _____ Tunnels   XXX- Narrow Road

_____Bad Banking Curves   _____Un-Even Pavement   _____Animal Xings

_____Pedestrians   XXX- Rd Shoulder Drop-Offs   XXX- Blind Curves

XXX- Water Run-Offs   XXX- Pavement Cracking   XXX- Rock Fall Areas

OVER ALL ROAD CONDITIONS: _____Ok _____Good XXX- Great _____Exc

Page 45

KY
Round Bottom
EC - SR30

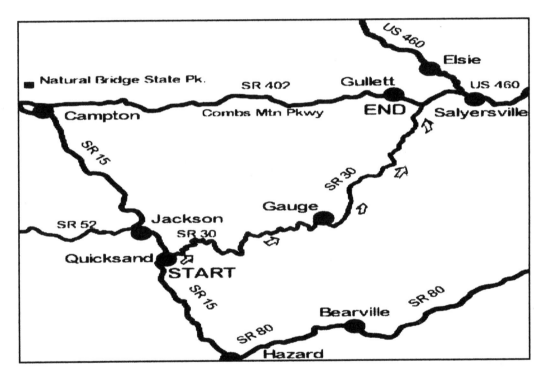

A great addition to a day's ride. It's hard to find roads with the quality of curves, and sweepers this run offers you. The flowing curves are hard to match. The corners are well balanced, and the run gives you a chance to test your limits. You'll enjoy the magic of this river run, as you make your way through the valley. The cornfields, deer, and mountain streams make this ride a country special. Hard to beat!

Road Evaluation

ROAD REFERENCE: **R#KY09 - ROUND BOTTOM**

RUN DISTANCE: 33- Miles

ELEVATION: 750- Ft > 1350- Ft

SPEED LIMITS: XXX- 15-25mph   XXX- 35mph   XXX- 45mph   XXX- 55mph   65+mph

RUN EVALUATION: _____Lots Of Fun // A Run To Remember

XXX- A Blast To Run // Plenty Of Curves

_____Great Run // Major Challenges

_____Extreme Ride // Surprises At Every Turn

TYPE OF ROAD:

XXX- Sweepers	XXX- Two Lane Traffic
XXX- Flowing Curves	_____Four Lane Traffic
XXX- Tight Curves	_____Scenic Overlooks / Views
_____Extreme Curves	_____National / State Parks

TYPE OF CURVES: XXX- Right Angles   XXX- Uies _____Zs   XXX- Ss

POSSIBLE ROAD HAZARDS:

_____Rain Grooves	_____Loose Gravel / Sand	_____Pot Holes
_____Slick Tar Spots	_____Tunnels	_____Narrow Road
_____Bad Banking Curves	_____Un-Even Pavement	_____Animal Xings
_____Pedestrians	XXX- Rd Shoulder Drop-Offs	_____Blind Curves
XXX- Water Run-Offs	XXX- Pavement Cracking	XXX- Rock Fall Areas

OVER ALL ROAD CONDITIONS: _____Ok   _____Good   _____Great   XXX- Exc

North Carolina
Twisties

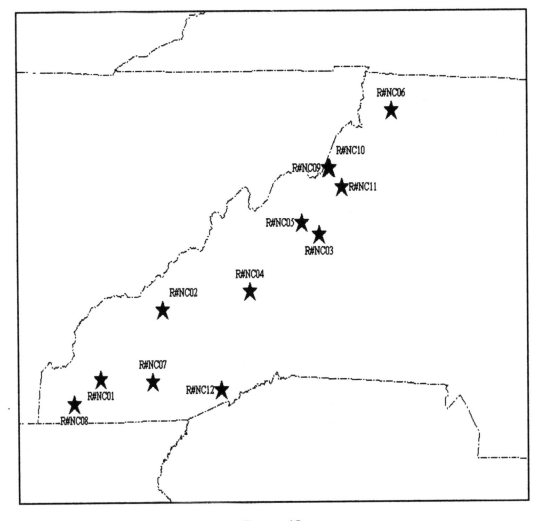

NORTH CAROLINA RUN LIST

RUN#NC01	NANTAHALA RIVER	(031MLS)	PG. 050
RUN#NC02	BLUE RIDGE PKWY WC/NC	(267MLS)	PG. 052
RUN#NC03	SANDY GAP LOOP	(017MLS)	PG. 054
RUN#NC04	DOGGETT GAP	(076MLS)	PG. 056
RUN#NC05	ROAN VALLEY	(088MLS)	PG. 058
RUN#NC06	PEAK VALLEY	(028MLS)	PG. 060
RUN#NC07	INDIAN GRAVE GAP	(056MLS)	PG. 062
RUN#NC08	COWEE GAP	(116MLS)	PG. 064
RUN#NC09	CRANBERRY / SPIVEY GAP	(072MLS)	PG. 066
RUN#NC10	LAUREL KNOB GAP	(044MLS)	PG. 068
RUN#NC11	ROUGH RIDGE	(065MLS)	PG. 070
RUN#NC12	PISGAH NATIONAL FOREST	(062MLS)	PG. 072

REFERENCE GUIDE
RUN SHEET
State ID
Run Name
State Map Location - Road ID
STATE MAP
Star Shows Run# (R#) Location

NC
Nantahala River
SW - SR1505/SR1401/SR1310

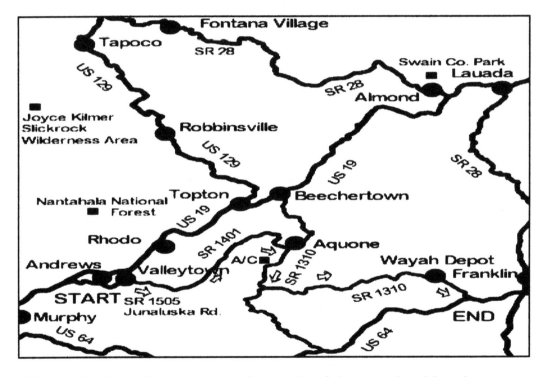

The run is short, but sweet, with a dash of danger. On this adventure, you will travel through valley sweepers, along the Nantahala River, and engage some very tight curves in the Nantahala National Forest. The fun starts at the Nantahala Dam where the road begins to narrow, and the curves become sharper. Check out the Appletree Campground for a good place to relax, and stay overnight. Great base camp area!

Road Evaluation

ROAD REFERENCE: **R#NC01 - NANTAHALA RIVER**

RUN DISTANCE: 31- Miles

ELEVATION: 1750- Ft > 4100- Ft

SPEED LIMITS: XXX- 15-25mph XXX- 35mph XXX- 45mph _____55mph _____65+mph

RUN EVALUATION: _____Lots Of Fun // A Run To Remember

XXX- A Blast To Run // Plenty Of Curves

_____Great Run // Major Challenges

_____Extreme Ride // Surprises at Every Turn

TYPE OF ROAD:

XXX- Sweepers	XXX- Two Lane Traffic
XXX- Flowing Curves	_____Four Lane Traffic
XXX- Tight Curves	_____Scenic Overlooks / Views
XXX- Extreme Curves	XXX- National / State Parks

TYPE OF CURVES: XXX- Right Angles   XXX- Uies   _____Zs   XXX- Ss

POSSIBLE ROAD HAZARDS:

_____Rain Grooves	XXX- Loose Gravel / Sand	_____Pot Holes
XXX- Slick Tar Spots	_____Tunnels	XXX- Narrow Road
_____Bad Banking Curves	_____ Un-Even Pavement	XXX- Animal Xings
_____Pedestrians	XXX- Rd Shoulder Drop-Offs	XXX- Blind Curves
XXX- Water Run-Offs	XXX- Pavement Cracking	XXX- Rock Fall Areas

OVER ALL ROAD CONDITIONS: _____Ok   XXX- Good   _____Great   _____Exc

NC
Blue Ridge Parkway
SW/NC

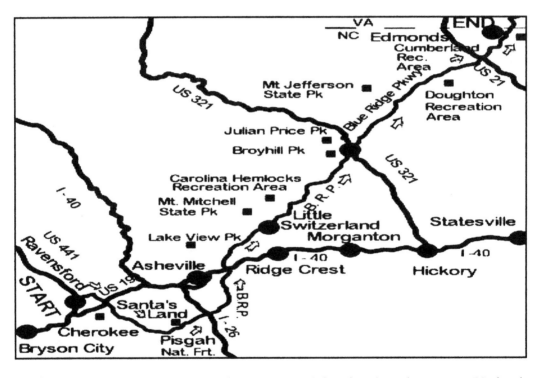

This has got to be the best known road in the Southeastern United States. A lot of folks just refer to it as the Parkway. It is known for its sweepers, and panoramic views. There are plenty of overlooks for you to enjoy the spectacular surrounds. Camping on the Parkway is permitted, but restricted to select areas. The road is constantly being patrolled, so check your speed. Great curves ahead; smooth and well banked!

Road Evaluation

ROAD REFERENCE: R#NC02 - BLUE RIDGE PARKWAY

RUN DISTANCE: 267- Miles

ELEVATION: 2000- Ft > 6100- Ft

SPEED LIMITS: XXX- 15-25mph XXX- 35mph XXX- 45mph _____55mph _____65+mph

RUN EVALUATION: _____Lots Of Fun // A Run To Remember

                           XXX- A Blast To Run // Plenty Of Curves

                           _____Great Run // Major Challenges

                           _____Extreme Ride // Surprises At Every Turn

TYPE OF ROAD: XXX- Sweepers   XXX- Two Lane Traffic

                           XXX- Flowing Curves   _____Four Lane Traffic

                           XXX- Tight Curves   XXX- Scenic Overlooks / Views

                           _____Extreme Curves   XXX- National / State Parks

TYPE OF CURVES: XXX- Right Angles   XXX- Uies _____Zs   XXX- Ss

**POSSIBLE ROAD
HAZARDS:**   XXX- Rain Grooves   XXX- Loose Gravel / Sand   _____Pot Holes

                           _____Slick Tar Spots   XXX- Tunnels   _____Narrow Road

                           _____Bad Banking Curves   _____Un-Even Pavement   XXX- Animal Xings

                           XXX- Pedestrians   XXX- Rd Shoulder Drop-Offs XXX- Blind Curves

                           XXX- Water Run-Offs   XXX- Pavement Cracking   XXX- Rock Fall Areas

**OVER ALL ROAD
CONDITIONS:**   _____Ok _____Good _____Great XXX- Exc

Page 53

NC
Sandy Gap Loop
WC - SR226A/SR226

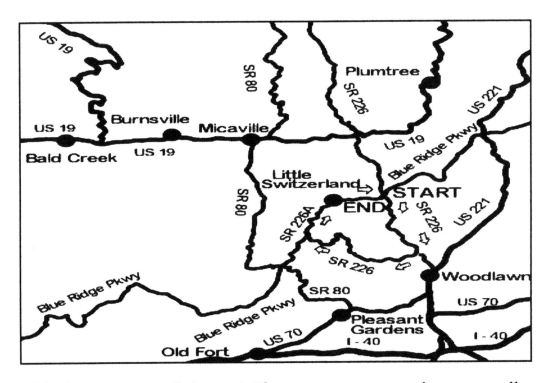

This is one sweet little run! If you want to experience a really awesome run, this one won't let you down. It's a road with all the right curves, and more than a few that will push you to the edge. From a downhill spiral of extreme curves, to a slow ride by a creek in the valley, you'll find this run makes the day. Being a complete loop, the run has one big problem; it's a little hard to stop. Continual fun!!!

Road Evaluation

ROAD REFERENCE: **R#NC03 - SANDY GAP LOOP**

RUN DISTANCE: 17- Miles

ELEVATION: 1350- Ft > 3200- Ft

SPEED LIMITS: XXX- 15-25mph XXX- 35mph XXX- 45mph _____55mph _____65+mph

RUN EVALUATION:
_____Lots Of Fun // A Run To Remember

_____A Blast To Run // Plenty Of Curves

_____Great Run // Major Challenges

XXX- Extreme Ride // Surprises At Every Turn

TYPE OF ROAD:

XXX- Sweepers	XXX- Two Lane Traffic
XXX- Flowing Curves	XXX- Four Lane Traffic
XXX- Tight Curves	XXX- Scenic Overlooks / Views
XXX- Extreme Curves	_____National / State Parks

TYPE OF CURVES: XXX- Right Angles XXX- Uies XXX- Zs XXX- Ss

POSSIBLE ROAD HAZARDS:

_____Rain Grooves	XXX- Loose Gravel / Sand	_____Pot Holes
_____Slick Tar Spots	_____Tunnels	XXX- Narrow Road
_____Bad Banking Curves	_____Un-Even Pavement	XXX- Animal Xings
XXX- Pedestrians	XXX- Rd Shoulder Drop-Offs	XXX- Blind Curves
XXX- Water Run-Offs	XXX- Pavement Cracking	XXX- Rock Fall Areas

OVER ALL ROAD CONDITIONS: _____Ok _____Good XXX- Great _____Exc

NC
Doggett Gap
WC-SR63/209/US25/SR208/212

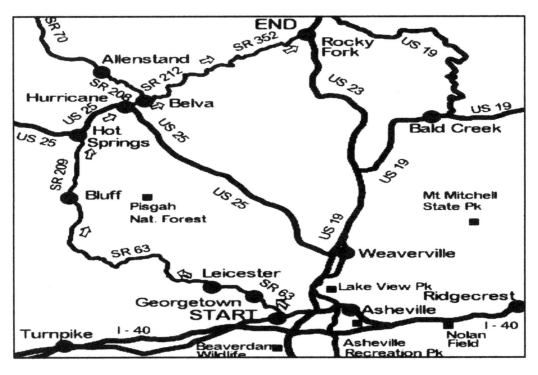

The SR63 valley run leads you along several mountain streams. Soon you will find yourself winding through the roads of the Pisgah National Forest. Leading to Hot Springs, there are a series of great curves to test your skills. After crossing the Blood River, you'll be heading to the Trail of the Lonesome Pine. Enjoy the fast flow of Shelton Laurel Creek following along the twisting roads, on your trip to Rocky Fork.

Road Evaluation

ROAD REFERENCE: R#NC04 - DOGGETT GAP

RUN DISTANCE: 76- Miles

ELEVATION: 1550- Ft > 4200- Ft

SPEED LIMITS: XXX- 15-25mph XXX- 35mph XXX- 45mph XXX- 55mph _____65+mph

RUN EVALUATION: _____Lots Of Fun // A Run To Remember

_____A Blast To Run // Plenty Of Curves

XXX- Great Run // Major Challenges

_____Extreme Ride // Surprises At Every Turn

TYPE OF ROAD:

XXX- Sweepers	XXX- Two Lane Traffic
XXX- Flowing Curves	XXX- Four Lane Traffic
XXX- Tight Curves	XXX- Scenic Overlooks / Views
XXX- Extreme Curves	XXX- National / State Parks

TYPE OF CURVES: XXX- Right Angles   XXX- Uies   XXX- Zs   XXX- Ss

POSSIBLE ROAD HAZARDS:

_____Rain Grooves	XXX- Loose Gravel / Sand	_____Pot Holes
XXX- Slick Tar Spots	_____Tunnels	XXX- Narrow Road
XXX- Bad Banking Curves	_____ Un-Even Pavement	_____Animal Xings
_____Pedestrians	XXX- Rd Shoulder Drop-Offs	XXX- Blind Curves
XXX- Water Run-Offs	_____Pavement Cracking	XXX- Rock Fall Areas

OVER ALL ROAD CONDITIONS: _____Ok _____Good XXX- Great _____Exc

NC / TN
Roan Valley
WC-SR80/SR226/SR261/SR143

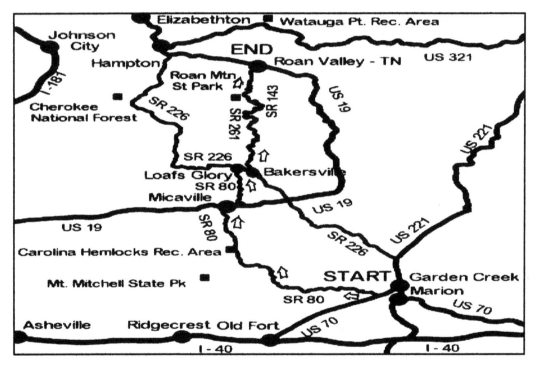

Few runs will have the views of Roan Mountain State Park. The roads going through the State Park are smooth, and challenging. Every type of curve you can imagine is on this run. Rambling through the Cherokee National Forest is not just fun, it's an experience. Take care on SR80, the curves can get pretty extreme. You'll find yourself in trouble before you know it. This entire run is a pleasure to travel. Time for fun!

Road Evaluation

ROAD REFERENCE: R#NC05 - ROAN VALLEY

RUN DISTANCE: 88- Miles

ELEVATION: 2450- Ft > 5500- Ft

SPEED LIMITS: XXX- 15-25mph XXX- 35mph XXX- 45mph XXX- 55mph _____65+mph

RUN EVALUATION: _____Lots Of Fun // A Run To Remember

   _____A Blast To Run // Plenty Of Curves

   _____Great Run // Major Challenges

   XXX-Extreme Ride // Surprises At Every Turn

TYPE OF ROAD: XXX- Sweepers   XXX- Two Lane Traffic

   XXX- Flowing Curves   _____Four Lane Traffic

   XXX- Tight Curves   XXX- Scenic Overlooks / Views

   XXX- Extreme Curves   XXX- National / State Parks

TYPE OF CURVES: XXX- Right Angles   XXX- Uies   _____Zs   XXX- Ss

POSSIBLE ROAD HAZARDS:

   _____Rain Grooves   XXX- Loose Gravel / Sand   _____Pot Holes

   _____Slick Tar Spots   _____Tunnels   XXX- Narrow Road

   XXX- Bad Banking Curves   _____ Un-Even Pavement   XXX- Animal Xings

   _____Pedestrians   XXX- Rd Shoulder Drop-Offs   XXX- Blind Curves

   XXX- Water Run-Offs   _____Pavement Cracking   XXX- Rock Fall Areas

OVER ALL ROAD CONDITIONS: _____Ok   _____Good   _____Great   XXX- Exc

NC
Peak Valley
NW - SR88

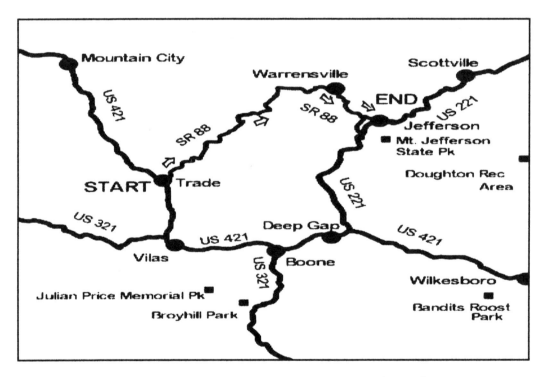

Just outside of Jefferson, NC, there is a beautiful, and fun little road to travel. The run combines valleys, rolling hills, rivers, heavy forest areas, and great mountain views. The Christmas trees covering the hillsides, give you a warm feeling as you're moving along this twisting highway. An old time power station on the North Fork New River, helps you remember the days past. Exciting curves for a little run!

Road Evaluation

ROAD REFERENCE: R#NC06 - PEAK VALLEY

RUN DISTANCE: 28- Miles

ELEVATION: 2700- Ft > 3660- Ft

SPEED LIMITS: _____15-25mph XXX- 35mph XXX- 45mph _____55mph _____65+mph

RUN EVALUATION: _____Lots Of Fun // A Run To Remember

XXX- A Blast To Run // Plenty Of Curves

_____Great Run // Major Challenges

_____Extreme Ride // Surprises At Every Turn

TYPE OF ROAD:

XXX- Sweepers	XXX- Two Lane Traffic
XXX- Flowing Curves	XXX- Four Lane Traffic
XXX- Tight Curves	XXX- Scenic Overlooks / Views
_____Extreme Curves	_____National / State Parks

TYPE OF CURVES: XXX- Right Angles   XXX- Uies   _____Zs   XXX- Ss

POSSIBLE ROAD HAZARDS:

_____Rain Grooves	XXX- Loose Gravel / Sand	_____Pot Holes
XXX- Slick Tar Spots	_____Tunnels	_____Narrow Road
_____Bad Banking Curves	_____Un-Even Pavement	_____Animal Xings
_____Pedestrians	XXX- Rd Shoulder Drop-Offs	XXX- Blind Curves
XXX- Water Run-Offs	XXX- Pavement Cracking	XXX- Rock Fall Areas

OVER ALL ROAD CONDITIONS: _____Ok XXX- Good _____Great _____Exc

NC
Indian Grave Gap
SW - SR28

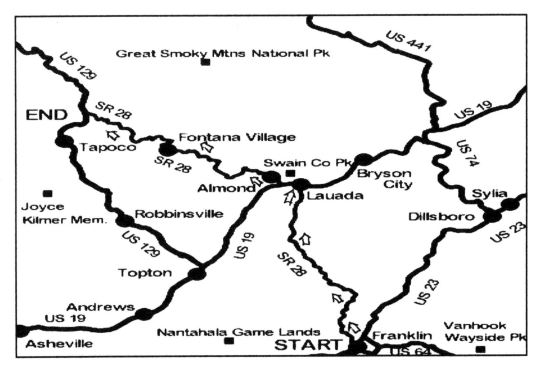

The Nantahala National Forest surrounds you with terrific views, as you're cruising along this great road. The Fontana Village Resort and Campground is worth checking out for an overnighter. You will find lots to do as you enjoy the Fontana Lake and Dam. Heavy on the twisties is the recipe for this run, as the road winds along the Little Tennessee River. The river is a perfect place to trout fish, or just cool your feet. What a day!

Road Evaluation

ROAD REFERENCE: R#NC07 - INDIAN GRAVE GAP

RUN DISTANCE: 56- Miles

ELEVATION: 1250- Ft > 2750- Ft

SPEED LIMITS: XXX- 15-25mph XXX- 35mph XXX- 45mph XXX- 55mph _____65+mph

RUN EVALUATION:

_____Lots Of Fun // A Run To Remember

_____A Blast To Run // Plenty Of Curves

XXX- Great Run // Major Challenges

_____Extreme Ride // Surprises At Every Turn

TYPE OF ROAD:

XXX- Sweepers	XXX- Two Lane Traffic
XXX- Flowing Curves	XXX- Four Lane Traffic
XXX- Tight Curves	XXX- Scenic Overlooks / Views
XXX- Extreme Curves	XXX- National / State Parks

TYPE OF CURVES: XXX- Right Angles   XXX- Uies   XXX- Zs   XXX- Ss

POSSIBLE ROAD HAZARDS:

_____Rain Grooves	_____Loose Gravel / Sand	_____Pot Holes
_____Slick Tar Spots	_____Tunnels	XXX- Narrow Road
_____Bad Banking Curves	_____Un-Even Pavement	XXX- Animal Xings
_____Pedestrians	XXX- Rd Shoulder Drop-Offs	XXX- Blind Curves
XXX- Water Run-Offs	XXX- Pavement Cracking	XXX- Rock Fall Areas

OVER ALL ROAD CONDITIONS: _____Ok _____Good XXX- Great _____Exc

NC
Cowee Gap
SW - US64

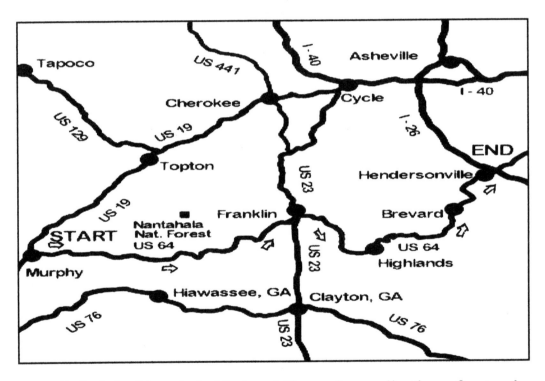

You'll find the Nantahala National Forest is a collection of nature's best of scenic views, and natural settings. This is a dream of a run. It has all the sweepers, and challenging twisties you can handle. The drop-offs along the road in the Highland area can get a little scary, so watch out. Waterfalls along the Cullasaja River are great, and make a good place to take a break. Relaxing once again!

Road Evaluation

ROAD REFERENCE: **R#NC08 - COWEE GAP**

RUN DISTANCE: 116- Miles

ELEVATION: 2150- Ft > 4100- Ft

SPEED LIMITS: XXX- 15-25mph XXX- 35mph XXX- 45mph XXX- 55mph _____65+mph

RUN EVALUATION: _____Lots Of Fun // A Run To Remember

_____A Blast To Run // Plenty Of Curves

_____Great Run // Major Challenges

XXX- Extreme Ride // Surprises At Every Turn

TYPE OF ROAD: XXX- Sweepers   XXX- Two Lane Traffic

XXX- Flowing Curves   XXX- Four Lane Traffic

XXX- Tight Curves   XXX- Scenic Overlooks / Views

XXX- Extreme Curves   XXX- National / State Parks

TYPE OF CURVES: XXX- Right Angles   XXX- Uies   _____Zs   XXX- Ss

POSSIBLE ROAD HAZARDS:

XXX- Rain Grooves	XXX- Loose Gravel / Sand	XXX- Pot Holes
XXX- Slick Tar Spots	_____Tunnels	XXX- Narrow Road
XXX- Bad Banking Curves	XXX- Un-Even Pavement	_____Animal Xings
XXX- Pedestrians	XXX- Rd Shoulder Drop-Offs	XXX- Blind Curves
XXX- Water Run-Offs	XXX- Pavement Cracking	XXX- Rock Fall Areas

OVER ALL ROAD CONDITIONS: _____Ok XXX- Good _____Great _____Exc

Page 65

NC - TN
Cranberry / Spivey Gap
NW/WC - US19E/US19W

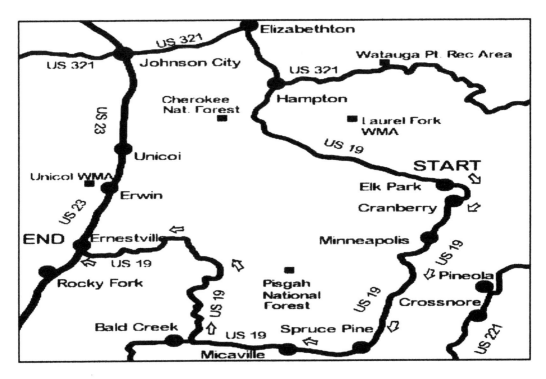

This run has numerous easy-going sweepers, blended with several series of tight corners. The road conditions are excellent, and will make for a comfortable ride. Journeying through the Pisgah National Forest is relaxing, but don't let those sharp corners surprise you. The run begins, and ends with a lot of great curves. There are a variety of places to enjoy in the small mountain towns of North Carolina.

Road Evaluation

ROAD REFERENCE: **R#NC09 - CRANBERRY / SPIVEYGAP**

RUN DISTANCE: 72- Miles

ELEVATION: 1950- Ft > 4050- Ft

SPEED LIMITS: XXX- 15-25mph   XXX- 35mph   XXX- 45mph   XXX- 55mph   _____65+mph

RUN EVALUATION: XXX- Lots Of Fun // A Run To Remember

     _____A Blast To Run // Plenty Of Curves

     _____Great Run // Major Challenges

     _____Extreme Ride // Surprises At Every Turn

TYPE OF ROAD:

XXX- Sweepers	XXX- Two Lane Traffic
XXX- Flowing Curves	XXX- Four Lane Traffic
XXX- Tight Curves	_____ Scenic Overlooks / Views
_____Extreme Curves	XXX- National / State Parks

TYPE OF CURVES: XXX- Right Angles   _____Uies   _____Zs   XXX- Ss

POSSIBLE ROAD HAZARDS:

_____Rain Grooves	XXX- Loose Gravel / Sand	_____Pot Holes
XXX- Slick Tar Spots	_____Tunnels	_____Narrow Road
_____Bad Banking Curves	_____Un-Even Pavement	XXX- Animal Xings
XXX- Pedestrians	XXX- Rd Shoulder Drop-Offs	_____Blind Curves
_____Water Run-Offs	XXX- Pavement Cracking	XXX- Rock Fall Areas

OVER ALL ROAD CONDITIONS: _____Ok   _____Good   _____Great   XXX- Exc

NC
Laurel Knob Gap
NW - SR194

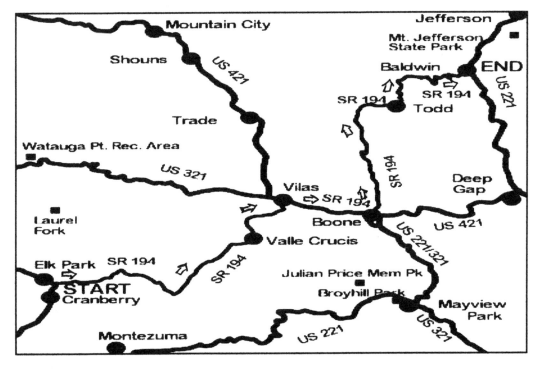

Picture yourself on the lazy curves of a shady road; highlighted with fenced meadows, a flowing creek, and Blue Spruce trees. Now imagine travelling through the heavily wooded hilltops on some twisties that get tighter by the mile. Well, if all this sounds good to you, I've got a run that might do the trick. Boone, NC, would be a good place to schedule a stop. It's great for shopping, or grabbing a bite to eat.

Road Evaluation

ROAD REFERENCE: **R#NC10 - LAUREL KNOB GAP**

RUN DISTANCE: 44- Miles

ELEVATION: 2650- Ft > 4200- Ft

SPEED LIMITS: XXX- 15-25mph XXX- 35mph XXX- 45mph XXX- 55mph _____65+mph

RUN EVALUATION: _____Lots Of Fun // A Run To Remember

XXX- A Blast To Run // Plenty Of Curves

_____Great Run // Major Challenges

_____Extreme Ride // Surprises at Every Turn

TYPE OF ROAD:

XXX- Sweepers	XXX- Two Lane Traffic
XXX- Flowing Curves	_____Four Lane Traffic
XXX- Tight Curves	XXX- Scenic Overlooks / Views
_____Extreme Curves	_____National / State Parks

TYPE OF CURVES: XXX- Right Angles XXX- Uies _____Zs XXX- Ss

POSSIBLE ROAD HAZARDS:

_____Rain Grooves	XXX- Loose Gravel / Sand	_____Pot Holes
_____Slick Tar Spots	_____Tunnels	_____Narrow Road
_____Bad Banking Curves	_____Un-Even Pavement	XXX- Animal Xings
XXX- Pedestrians	XXX- Rd Shoulder Drop-Offs	XXX- Blind Curves
_____Water Run-Offs	XXX- Pavement Cracking	_____Rock Fall Areas

OVER ALL ROAD CONDITIONS: _____Ok _____Good XXX- Great _____Exc

NC
Rough Ridge
NW - US221

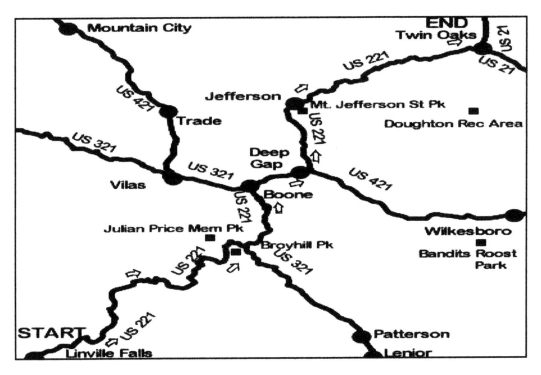

It's dip and twist on the old NC State Byway. From an open valley bottom run along the South Fork New River, to some heavily wooded roads around the Mount Jefferson State Park, you will enjoy the diversity of this run. The continuous "S" curves streaking around Grandfather Mountain make this run a major challenge. The Blue Ridge Parkway intersects the road several times, so a few side trips might be nice.

Road Evaluation

ROAD REFERENCE: **R#NC11 - ROUGH RIDGE**

RUN DISTANCE: 65- Miles

ELEVATION: 2900- Ft > 4850- Ft

SPEED LIMITS: XXX- 15-25mph XXX- 35mph XXX- 45mph XXX- 55mph _____65+mph

RUN EVALUATION: _____Lots Of Fun // A Run To Remember

_____A Blast To Run // Plenty Of Curves

XXX- Great Run // Major Challenges

_____Extreme Ride // Surprises At Every Turn

TYPE OF ROAD:

XXX- Sweepers	XXX- Two Lane Traffic
XXX- Flowing Curves	XXX- Four Lane Traffic
XXX- Tight Curves	XXX- Scenic Overlooks / Views
_____Extreme Curves	XXX- National / State Parks

TYPE OF CURVES: XXX- Right Angles XXX- Uies XXX- Zs XXX- Ss

POSSIBLE ROAD HAZARDS:

_____Rain Grooves	XXX- Loose Gravel / Sand	XXX- Pot Holes
_____Slick Tar Spots	_____Tunnels	_____Narrow Road
_____Bad Banking Curves	_____Un-Even Pavement	XXX- Animal Xings
_____Pedestrians	XXX- Rd Shoulder Drop-Offs	XXX- Blind Curves
XXX- Water Run-Offs	XXX- Pavement Cracking	XXX- Rock Fall Areas

OVER ALL ROAD CONDITIONS: _____Ok XXX- Good _____Great _____Exc

NC
Pisgah National Forest
SW - SR215/US276

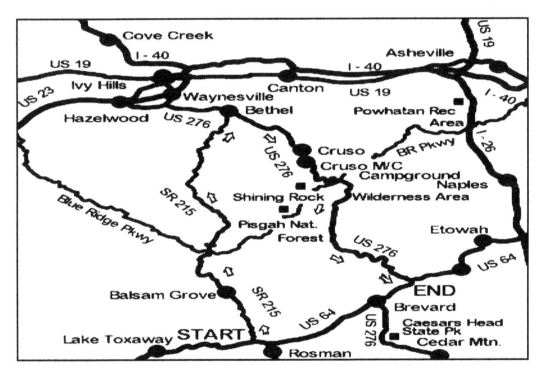

Put this run at the top of your list. The combination of these roads is terrific, allowing you to enjoy every type of curve you can imagine. It intersects the Blue Ridge Parkway twice, changing elevations numerous times, and surrounding you with fantastic views. You will find the Cruso M/C campground makes a great base camp for your daily road trips. It is located right off the Parkway among some great NC twisties.

Road Evaluation

ROAD REFERENCE: R#NC12 - PISGAH NATIONAL FORREST

RUN DISTANCE: 62- Miles

ELEVATION: 2150- Ft > 5200- Ft

SPEED LIMITS: XXX- 15-25mph XXX- 35mph XXX- 45mph XXX- 55mph _____65+mph

RUN EVALUATION:

_____Lots Of Fun // A Run To Remember

_____A Blast To Run // Plenty Of Curves

XXX- Great Run // Major Challenges

_____Extreme Ride // Surprises At Every Turn

TYPE OF ROAD:

XXX- Sweepers	XXX- Two Lane Traffic
XXX- Flowing Curves	_____Four Lane Traffic
XXX- Tight Curves	XXX- Scenic Overlooks / Views
XXX- Extreme Curves	XXX- National / State Parks

TYPE OF CURVES: XXX- Right Angles   XXX- Uies   XXX- Zs   XXX- Ss

POSSIBLE ROAD HAZARDS:

_____Rain Grooves	_____Loose Gravel / Sand	_____Pot Holes
XXX- Slick Tar Spots	_____Tunnels	XXX- Narrow Road
XXX- Bad Banking Curves	_____Un-Even Pavement	_____Animal Xings
XXX- Pedestrians	XXX- Rd Shoulder Drop-Offs	XXX- Blind Curves
XXX- Water Run-Offs	XXX- Pavement Cracking	XXX- Rock Fall Areas

OVER ALL ROAD CONDITIONS: _____Ok _____Good XXX- Great _____Exc

Page 73

TENNESSEE
Twisties

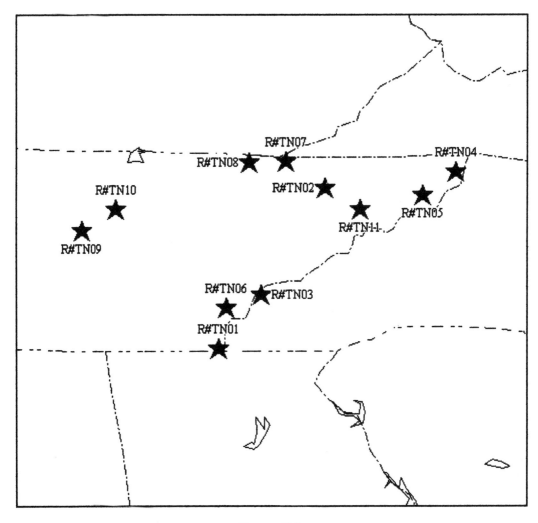

TENNESSEE RUN LIST

REFERENCE GUIDE
RUN SHEET
State ID
Run Name
State Map Location - Road ID
STATE MAP
Star Shows Run# (R#) Location

TN
Mac Point Loop
SE - US64/SR30/315/39/SR68

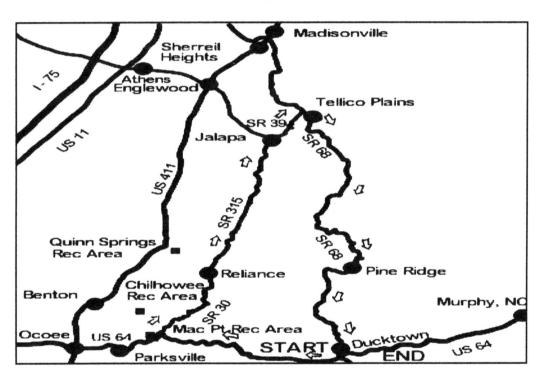

Surrounded by the Cherokee National Forest, you will start the run off riding along the Oconee River. This is a great recreational area for rafting, fishing, biking, and hiking. Trout fishing is great around the Hiwassee River Bridge off SR315. The road conditions on this run are excellent. There are continuous twisties with an abundance of "S" curves, some of the best around. Beware of the blind curves; they can be tricky.

Road Evaluation

ROAD REFERENCE: **R#TN01 - MAC POINT LOOP**

RUN DISTANCE: 75- Miles

ELEVATION: 800- Ft > 1650- Ft

SPEED LIMITS: XXX- 15-25mph XXX- 35mph XXX- 45mph XXX- 55mph _____65+mph

RUN EVALUATION: _____Lots Of Fun // A Run To Remember

XXX- A Blast To Run // Plenty Of Curves

_____Great Run // Major Challenges

_____Extreme Ride // Surprises At Every Turn

TYPE OF ROAD:

XXX- Sweepers	XXX- Two Lane Traffic
XXX- Flowing Curves	XXX- Four Lane Traffic
XXX- Tight Curves	XXX- Scenic Overlooks / Views
_____Extreme Curves	XXX- National / State Parks

TYPE OF CURVES: XXX- Right Angles _____Uies _____Zs XXX- Ss

POSSIBLE ROAD HAZARDS:

_____Rain Grooves	_____Loose Gravel / Sand	_____Pot Holes
_____Slick Tar Spots	_____Tunnels	XXX- Narrow Road
_____Bad Banking Curves	_____Un-Even Pavement	XXX- Animal Xings
XXX- Pedestrians	XXX- Rd Shoulder Drop-Offs	XXX- Blind Curves
_____Water Run-Offs	_____Pavement Cracking	XXX- Rock Fall Areas

OVER ALL ROAD CONDITIONS: _____Ok _____Good _____Great XXX- Exc

TN
Big War Gap
NE - SR31/SR66

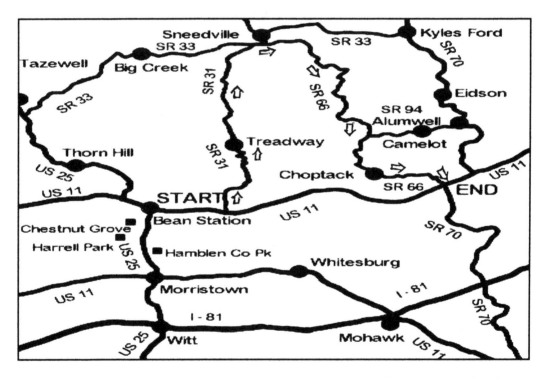

Starting out along the Holston River you'll soon find yourself spiraling through the curves of one mighty fine run. The views, rivers, and roads provide a terrific road trip. Few roads offer the challenges this run has in store for you. The great variety of curves adds to this run's excitement. As the road narrows, the curves tighten, and your pulse quickens. It's easy to get over your head if you're not careful. Savor this one!

Road Evaluation

ROAD REFERENCE: **R#TN02 - BIG WAR GAP**

RUN DISTANCE: 42- Miles

ELEVATION: 1050- Ft > 1850- Ft

SPEED LIMITS: XXX- 15-25mph XXX- 35mph XXX- 45mph XXX- 55mph _____65+mph

RUN EVALUATION:
_____Lots Of Fun // A Run To Remember

_____A Blast To Run // Plenty Of Curves

_____Great Run // Major Challenges

XXX- Extreme Ride // Surprises At Every Turn

TYPE OF ROAD:

XXX- Sweepers	XXX- Two Lane Traffic
XXX- Flowing Curves	_____Four Lane Traffic
XXX- Tight Curves	XXX- Scenic Overlooks / Views
XXX- Extreme Curves	_____National / State Parks

TYPE OF CURVES: XXX- Right Angles   XXX- Uies   XXX- Zs   XXX- Ss

POSSIBLE ROAD HAZARDS:

_____Rain Grooves	XXX- Loose Gravel / Sand	_____Pot Holes
_____Slick Tar Spots	_____Tunnels	XXX- Narrow Road
_____Bad Banking Curves	_____Un-Even Pavement	XXX- Animal Xings
_____Pedestrians	XXX- Rd Shoulder Drop-Offs	XXX- Blind Curves
XXX- Water Run-Offs	_____Pavement Cracking	XXX- Rock Fall Areas

OVER ALL ROAD CONDITIONS: _____Ok   _____Good   _____Great   XXX- Exc

TN / NC
Deals Gap
SE - US129/Foothills Parkway

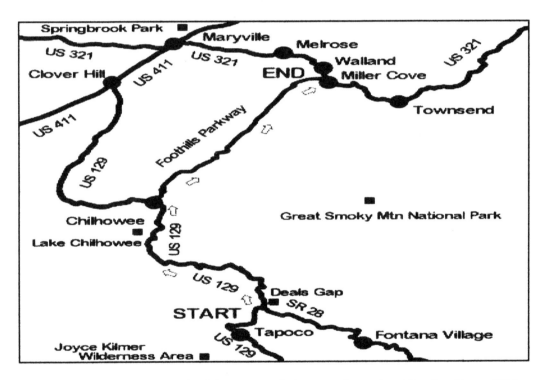

The word Exxxtreme holds a special meaning for Deals Gap. This section of the run has 318 curves in 11 ½ miles, and you will find yourself more than a little challenged to finish it. After pushing your limits on Deals Gap, relax by the shores of Lake Chihowee. At the lake, you can connect with the Foothills Parkway. A beautiful road with wide sweepers, lazy curves, and panoramic views. Run of Runs! For a great sandwich stop in at Crossroads of Time on the NC border.

Road Evaluation

ROAD REFERENCE: R#TN03 - DEALS GAP

RUN DISTANCE: 32- Miles

ELEVATION: 850- Ft > 2300- Ft

SPEED LIMITS: XXX- 15-25mph   XXX- 35mph   XXX- 45mph   _____55mph   _____65+mph

RUN EVALUATION:

_____Lots Of Fun // A Run To Remember

_____A Blast To Run // Plenty Of Curves

_____Great Run // Major Challenges

XXX- Extreme Ride // Surprises At Every Turn

TYPE OF ROAD:

XXX- Sweepers	XXX- Two Lane Traffic
XXX- Flowing Curves	_____Four Lane Traffic
XXX- Tight Curves	XXX- Scenic Overlooks / Views
XXX- Extreme Curves	XXX- National / State Parks

TYPE OF CURVES: XXX- Right Angles   XXX- Uies   XXX- Zs   XXX- Ss

POSSIBLE ROAD HAZARDS:

_____Rain Grooves	XXX- Loose Gravel / Sand	_____Pot Holes
_____Slick Tar Spots	_____Tunnels	XXX- Narrow Road
XXX- Bad Banking Curves	_____Un-Even Pavement	_____Animal Xings
_____Pedestrians	XXX- Rd Shoulder Drop-Offs	XXX- Blind Curves
XXX- Water Run-Offs	_____Pavement Cracking	XXX- Rock Fall Areas

OVER ALL ROAD CONDITIONS: _____Ok   _____Good   _____Great   XXX- Exc

TN
Shady Valley
NE - US421

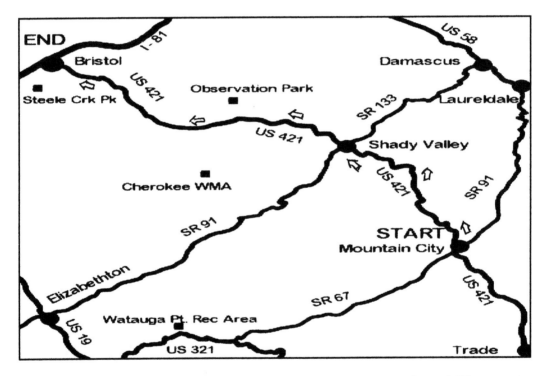

A must for twistie lovers. You'll quickly be into a serious hilltop run, stretching through the Cherokee National Forest. Now get ready to be intimidated by a set of killer curves. From these curves, you will drop into a valley with a view made in heaven. Shady Valley is a picture book town encircled by beautiful majestic mountains. As you leave the valley, get ready to push your limits. Exxxtreme curves ahead!!!

Road Evaluation

ROAD REFERENCE: **R#TN04 - SHADY VALLEY**

RUN DISTANCE: 31- Miles

ELEVATION: 1600- Ft > 3900- Ft

SPEED LIMITS: XXX- 15-25mph XXX- 35mph XXX- 45mph XXX- 55mph _____65+mph

RUN EVALUATION:
_____Lots Of Fun // A Run To Remember

_____A Blast To Run // Plenty Of Curves

_____Great Run // Major Challenges

XXX- Extreme Ride // Surprises At Every Turn

TYPE OF ROAD:

XXX- Sweepers	XXX- Two Lane Traffic
XXX- Flowing Curves	XXX- Four Lane Traffic
XXX- Tight Curves	XXX- Scenic Overlooks / Views
XXX- Extreme Curves	XXX- National / State Parks

TYPE OF CURVES: XXX- Right Angles   XXX- Uies   XXX- Zs   XXX- Ss

POSSIBLE ROAD HAZARDS:

_____Rain Grooves	XXX- Loose Gravel / Sand	_____Pot Holes
_____Slick Tar Spots	_____Tunnels	_____Narrow Road
_____Bad Banking Curves	_____Un-Even Pavement	_____Animal Xings
_____Pedestrians	XXX- Rd Shoulder Drop-Offs	XXX- Blind Curves
XXX- Water Run-Offs	_____Pavement Cracking	XXX- Rock Fall Areas

OVER ALL ROAD CONDITIONS: _____Ok _____Good _____Great XXX- Exc

TN - NC
Watauga Point
NE - US321

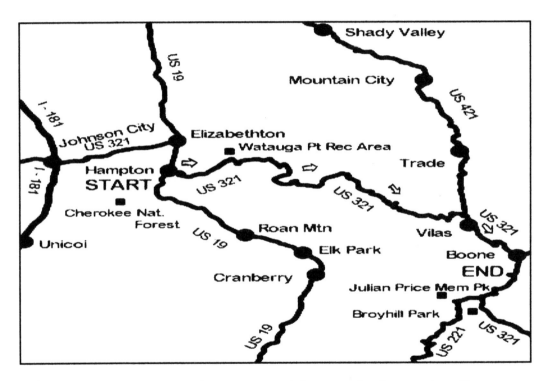

Fantastic Scenic Lake views, great lake overlooks, and valleys surrounded by rolling hills, make this run one of a kind. You might make time for a refreshing stop at Laurel Falls in the Cherokee National Forest. All in all, this is a splendid lake run that definitely should be added to your travel plans. Sweepers and flowing curves are the highlight of this run. The road and scenery are a perfect blend for that special trip.

Road Evaluation

ROAD REFERENCE: **R#TN05 - WATAUGA POINT**

RUN DISTANCE: 40- Miles

ELEVATION: 1850- Ft > 3050- Ft

SPEED LIMITS: XXX- 15-25mph XXX- 35mph XXX- 45mph XXX- 55mph _____65+mph

RUN EVALUATION: _____Lots Of Fun // A Run To Remember

XXX- A Blast To Run // Plenty Of Curves

_____Great Run // Major Challenges

_____Extreme Ride // Surprises At Every Turn

TYPE OF ROAD:

XXX- Sweepers	XXX- Two Lane Traffic
XXX- Flowing Curves	_____Four Lane Traffic
XXX- Tight Curves	XXX- Scenic Overlooks / Views
_____Extreme Curves	XXX- National / State Parks

TYPE OF CURVES: XXX- Right Angles   XXX- Uies   _____Zs   XXX- Ss

POSSIBLE ROAD HAZARDS:

_____Rain Grooves	XXX- Loose Gravel / Sand	_____Pot Holes
_____Slick Tar Spots	_____Tunnels	_____Narrow Road
_____Bad Banking Curves	_____Un-Even Pavement	XXX- Animal Xings
XXX- Pedestrians	XXX- Rd Shoulder Drop-Offs	_____Blind Curves
_____Water Run-Offs	XXX- Pavement Cracking	XXX- Rock Fall Areas

OVER ALL ROAD CONDITIONS: _____Ok _____Good XXX- Great _____Exc

Page 85

TN - NC
Cherohala Skyway
SE - SR360/SR165/SR143

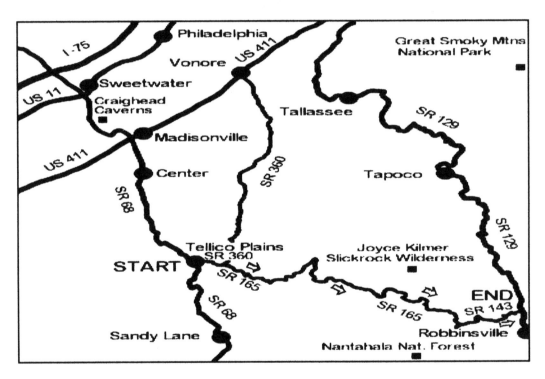

The Cherohala Skyway completed in 1997, makes the connection between Tennessee, and North Carolina. This Scenic Byway combines the beauty of both the Cherokee, and Nantahala National Forests. You can enjoy trout fishing on the Tellico River, or hiking the Warrior Passage Trail. Fantastic views, excellent roads, continuous "S" curves, and lazy sweepers highlight this run. There are plenty of great places to stop.

Road Evaluation

ROAD REFERENCE: **R#TN06 - CHEROHALA SKYWAY**

RUN DISTANCE: 53- Miles

ELEVATION: 1100- Ft > 5400- Ft

SPEED LIMITS: XXX- 15-25mph XXX- 35mph XXX- 45mph _____55mph _____65+mph

RUN EVALUATION: _____Lots Of Fun // A Run To Remember

XXX- A Blast To Run // Plenty Of Curves

_____Great Run // Major Challenges

_____Extreme Ride // Surprises At Every Turn

TYPE OF ROAD:

XXX- Sweepers	XXX- Two Lane Traffic
XXX- Flowing Curves	_____Four Lane Traffic
XXX- Tight Curves	XXX- Scenic Overlooks / Views
_____Extreme Curves	XXX- National / State Parks

TYPE OF CURVES: XXX- Right Angles _____Uies _____Zs XXX- Ss

POSSIBLE ROAD HAZARDS:

_____Rain Grooves	XXX- Loose Gravel / Sand	_____Pot Holes
_____Slick Tar Spots	_____Tunnels	_____Narrow Road
XXX- Bad Banking Curves	_____Un-Even Pavement	_____Animal Xings
XXX- Pedestrians	_____Rd Shoulder Drop-Offs	XXX- Blind Curves
_____Water Run-Offs	_____Pavement Cracking	XXX- Rock Fall Areas

OVER ALL ROAD CONDITIONS: _____Ok _____Good _____Great XXX- Exc

TN
Powell River
NE - SR63

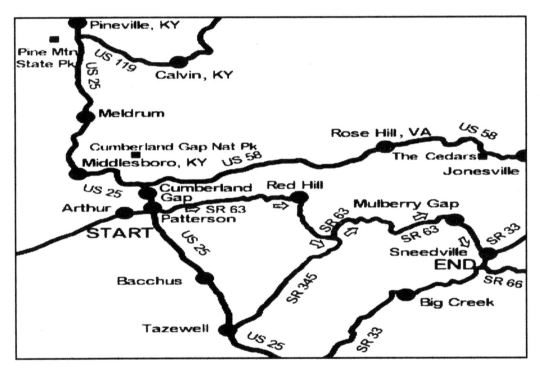

Here's a road that combines a beautiful valley run with some excellent cornering in the shady hills. With an abundance of dip and twist cornering, it is wise to be cautious on this road. Keep an eye out for the farm animal crossings. You'll find the locals to be quite social, as they seemed eager to extend a friendly smile, and wave to strangers. The scenic valley views make this run complete. Very enjoyable ride!!!

Road Evaluation

ROAD REFERENCE: **R#TN07 - POWELL RIVER**

RUN DISTANCE: 37- Miles

ELEVATION: 1200- Ft > 2100- Ft

SPEED LIMITS: XXX- 15-25mph   XXX- 35mph   XXX- 45mph   _____55mph   _____65+mph

RUN EVALUATION: _____Lots Of Fun // A Run To Remember

                        _____A Blast To Run // Plenty Of Curves

                        XXX- Great Run // Major Challenges

                        _____Extreme Ride // Surprises At Every Turn

TYPE OF ROAD: XXX- Sweepers   XXX- Two Lane Traffic

                        XXX- Flowing Curves   _____Four Lane Traffic

                        XXX- Tight Curves   XXX- Scenic Overlooks / Views

                        XXX- Extreme Curves   _____National / State Parks

TYPE OF CURVES: XXX- Right Angles   XXX- Uies   _____Zs   XXX- Ss

POSSIBLE ROAD HAZARDS:

_____Rain Grooves	XXX- Loose Gravel / Sand	_____Pot Holes
_____Slick Tar Spots	_____Tunnels	XXX- Narrow Road
XXX- Bad Banking Curves	_____Un-Even Pavement	XXX- Animal Xings
_____Pedestrians	XXX- Rd Shoulder Drop-Offs	XXX- Blind Curves
XXX- Water Run-Offs	XXX- Pavement Cracking	XXX- Rock Fall Areas

OVER ALL ROAD CONDITIONS: _____Ok   _____Good   XXX- Great   _____Exc

TN - KY
Hickory Hill
NE - SR90(TN) / SR74(KY)

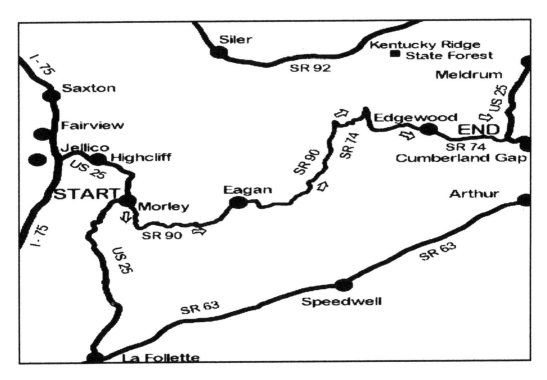

Shady mountain roads, extreme curves, and plenty of "S" cornering highlight this run. You will find the area heavily wooded, with creeks flowing through pastures surrounded by beautiful rolling hills. This is a fantastic collection of challenging curves; the dip and twist variety. If you are looking for the thrill of tight cornering, this run will make your day. Nature's best in scenic views for this choice run!

Road Evaluation

ROAD REFERENCE: **R#TN08 - HICKORY HILL**

RUN DISTANCE: 47- Miles

ELEVATION: 950- Ft > 2330- Ft

SPEED LIMITS: XXX- 15-25mph XXX- 35mph XXX- 45mph _____55mph _____65+mph

RUN EVALUATION:
_____Lots Of Fun // A Run To Remember

_____A Blast To Run // Plenty Of Curves

XXX- Great Run // Major Challenges

_____Extreme Ride // Surprises At Every Turn

TYPE OF ROAD:

XXX- Sweepers	XXX- Two Lane Traffic
XXX- Flowing Curves	_____Four Lane Traffic
XXX- Tight Curves	XXX- Scenic Overlooks / Views
XXX- Extreme Curves	_____National / State Parks

TYPE OF CURVES: XXX- Right Angles   XXX- Uies   XXX- Zs   XXX- Ss

POSSIBLE ROAD HAZARDS:

_____Rain Grooves	XXX- Loose Gravel / Sand	XXX- Pot Holes
_____Slick Tar Spots	_____Tunnels	XXX- Narrow Road
XXX- Bad Banking Curves	XXX- Un-Even Pavement	_____Animal Xings
_____Pedestrians	XXX- Rd Shoulder Drop-Offs	XXX- Blind Curves
XXX- Water Run-Offs	XXX- Pavement Cracking	XXX- Rock Fall Areas

OVER ALL ROAD CONDITIONS: _____Ok _____Good XXX- Great _____Exc

TN
Center Hill Lake
NC - SR96/SR141/SR56

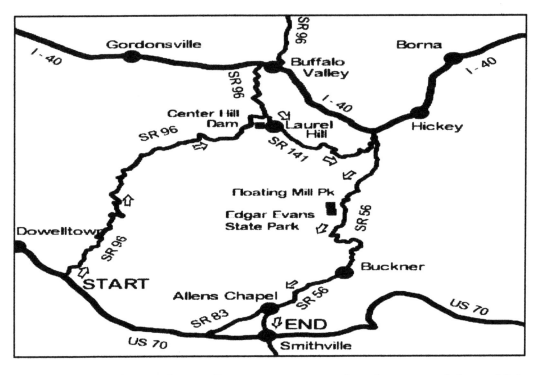

The wide variety of excellent curves, scenic views, and beautiful recreational areas make this run a pleasure for everyone. Riding across the Center Hill Dam, you'll enjoy overlooking the Caney River, and Center Hill Lake. For a little break, or some hiking, consider a stop at Edgar Evans State Park. Further south on SR56, you can find several serious sweepers, and tight snaking curves in the hills of Beersheba Springs.

Road Evaluation

ROAD REFERENCE: **R#TN09 - CENTER HILL LAKE**

RUN DISTANCE: 37- Miles

ELEVATION: 650- Ft > 1920- Ft

SPEED LIMITS: XXX- 15-25mph XXX- 35mph XXX- 45mph XXX- 55mph _____65+mph

RUN EVALUATION: _____Lots Of Fun // A Run To Remember

    _____A Blast To Run // Plenty Of Curves

    XXX- Great Run // Major Challenges

    _____Extreme Ride // Surprises At Every Turn

TYPE OF ROAD:

XXX- Sweepers	XXX- Two Lane Traffic
XXX- Flowing Curves	_____Four Lane Traffic
XXX- Tight Curves	XXX- Scenic Overlooks / Views
XXX- Extreme Curves	XXX- National / State Parks

TYPE OF CURVES: XXX- Right Angles   XXX- Uies   XXX- Zs   XXX- Ss

POSSIBLE ROAD HAZARDS:

XXX- Rain Grooves	XXX- Loose Gravel / Sand	_____Pot Holes
_____Slick Tar Spots	_____Tunnels	_____Narrow Road
XXX- Bad Banking Curves	XXX- Un-Even Pavement	_____Animal Xings
_____Pedestrians	XXX- Rd Shoulder Drop-Offs	XXX- Blind Curves
XXX- Water Run-Offs	XXX- Pavement Cracking	XXX- Rock Fall Areas

OVER ALL ROAD CONDITIONS: _____Ok _____Good XXX- Great _____Exc

TN
Roaring River
NC - SR135/SR56

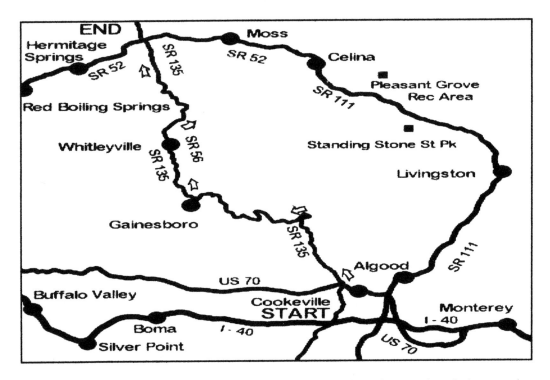

This country road special is highlighted with fantastic right angle curves. The dip and twist cornering provides an exciting way to pass the afternoon. Surrounded by rolling hills, fenced pastures, and rural farms, you'll enjoy travelling along the Cumberland River. The Roaring River Recreational Area offers a great place to take a break. Picnic and relax, it's going to be a fine day to play.

Road Evaluation

ROAD REFERENCE: **R#TN10 - ROARING RIVER**

RUN DISTANCE: 46- Miles

ELEVATION: 450- Ft > 1150- Ft

SPEED LIMITS: XXX- 15-25mph XXX- 35mph XXX- 45mph XXX- 55mph _____65+mph

RUN EVALUATION: _____Lots Of Fun // A Run To Remember

XXX- A Blast To Run // Plenty Of Curves

_____Great Run // Major Challenges

_____Extreme Ride // Surprises At Every Turn

TYPE OF ROAD:

XXX- Sweepers	XXX- Two Lane Traffic
XXX- Flowing Curves	_____Four Lane Traffic
XXX- Tight Curves	XXX- Scenic Overlooks / Views
_____Extreme Curves	XXX- National / State Parks

TYPE OF CURVES: XXX- Right Angles   XXX- Uies   _____Zs   XXX- Ss

POSSIBLE ROAD HAZARDS:

_____Rain Grooves	XXX- Loose Gravel / Sand	XXX- Pot Holes
XXX- Slick Tar Spots	_____Tunnels	_____Narrow Road
_____Bad Banking Curves	XXX- Un-Even Pavement	XXX- Animal Xings
_____Pedestrians	XXX- Rd Shoulder Drop-Offs	XXX- Blind Curves
XXX- Water Run-Offs	XXX- Pavement Cracking	XXX- Rock Fall Areas

OVER ALL ROAD CONDITIONS: _____Ok   XXX- Good   _____Great   _____Exc

TN
Little War Gap
NE - SR70

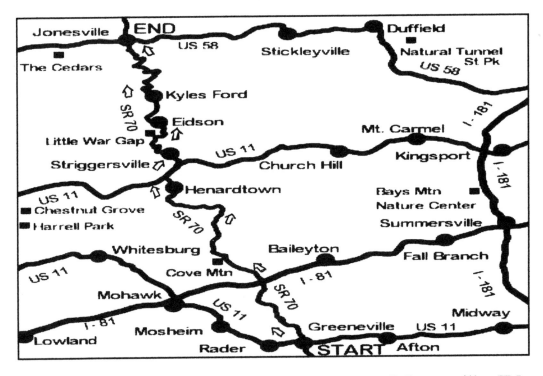

Welcome to the Lonesome Pine Trail. Just out of Greeneville, TN, you'll be travelling on a beautiful valley run. This area is covered with horse, and cattle farms. Relax and enjoy the sites of the Holston, Clinch, and Powell Rivers. Sweepers will make way for tighter curves near Cove Mountain. After Rogersville, the fun starts at Little War Gap, with some terrific curves, and continues into Kentucky.

Road Evaluation

ROAD REFERENCE: R#TN11 - LITTLE WAR GAP

RUN DISTANCE: 61- Miles

ELEVATION: 1100- Ft > 1800- Ft

SPEED LIMITS: XXX- 15-25mph XXX- 35mph XXX- 45mph XXX- 55mph _____65+mph

RUN EVALUATION: _____Lots Of Fun // A Run To Remember

    _____A Blast To Run // Plenty Of Curves

    XXX- Great Run // Major Challenges

    _____Extreme Ride // Surprises At Every Turn

TYPE OF ROAD:

XXX- Sweepers	XXX- Two Lane Traffic
XXX- Flowing Curves	XXX- Four Lane Traffic
XXX- Tight Curves	XXX- Scenic Overlooks / Views
_____Extreme Curves	_____National / State Parks

TYPE OF CURVES: XXX- Right Angles XXX- Uies _____Zs XXX- Ss

POSSIBLE ROAD HAZARDS:

_____Rain Grooves	XXX- Loose Gravel / Sand	XXX- Pot Holes
_____Slick Tar Spots	_____Tunnels	_____Narrow Road
_____Bad Banking Curves	_____Un-Even Pavement	_____Animal Xings
_____Pedestrians	XXX- Rd Shoulder Drop-Offs	XXX- Blind Curves
_____Water Run-Offs	XXX- Pavement Cracking	XXX- Rock Fall Areas

OVER ALL ROAD CONDITIONS: _____Ok _____Good XXX- Great _____Exc

VIRGINIA
Twisties

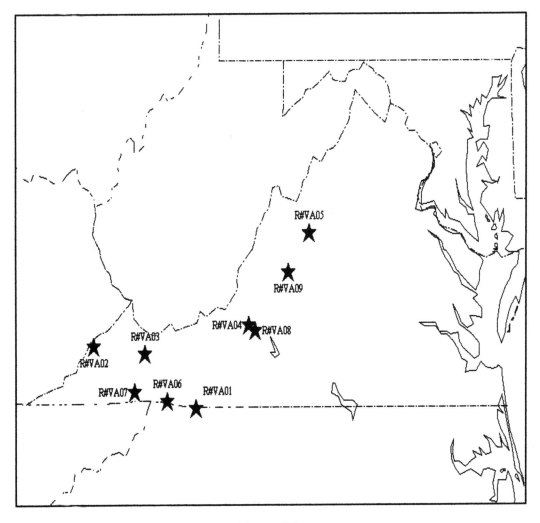

VIRGINIA RUN LIST

REFERENCE GUIDE
RUN SHEET
State ID
Run Name
State Map Location - Road ID
STATE MAP
Star Shows Run# (R#) Location

VA
SW - Blue Ridge Pkwy
NC - Skyline Drive

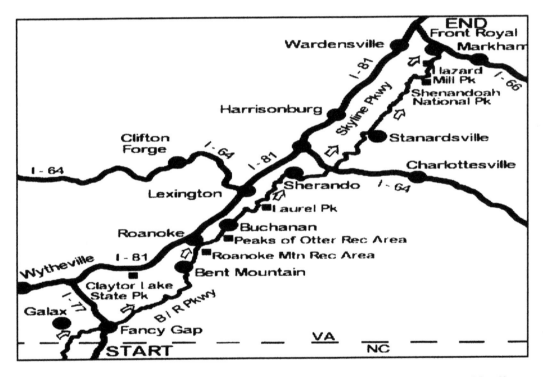

Start out on the Blue Ridge Parkway, and make your way to Skyline Drive, riding through the Shenandoah National Park. Your travels allow you to appreciate the awesome beauty, and natural settings of the mountains. The panoramic views will be a delight for every traveler. There are plenty of scenic overlooks along the way to enjoy the surroundings. Fall offers an amazing array of leaf colors. A must for all!

Road Evaluation

ROAD REFERENCE: **R#VA01 - BLUE RIDGE PARKWAY / SKYLINE DRIVE**

RUN DISTANCE: 307- Miles

ELEVATION: 750- Ft > 3850- Ft

SPEED LIMITS: XXX- 15-25mph XXX- 35mph XXX- 45mph _____55mph _____65+mph

RUN EVALUATION: XXX- Lots Of Fun // A Run To Remember

_____Blast To Run // Plenty Of Curves

_____Great Run // Major Challenges

_____Extreme Ride // Surprises at Every Turn

TYPE OF ROAD:

XXX- Sweepers	XXX- Two Lane Traffic
XXX- Flowing Curves	_____Four Lane Traffic
XXX-Tight Curves	XXX- Scenic Overlooks / Views
_____Extreme Curves	XXX- National / State Parks

TYPE OF CURVES: XXX- Right Angles _____Uies _____Zs XXX- Ss

POSSIBLE ROAD HAZARDS:

XXX- Rain Grooves	XXX- Loose Gravel / Sand	XXX- Pot Holes
XXX- Slick Tar Spots	XXX- Tunnels	_____Narrow Road
XXX- Bad Banking Curves	XXX- Un-Even Pavement	XXX- Animal Xings
XXX- Pedestrians	XXX- Rd Shoulder Drop-Offs	_____Blind Curves
XXX- Water Run-Offs	XXX- Pavement Cracking	XXX- Rock Fall Areas

OVER ALL ROAD CONDITIONS: _____Ok _____Good XXX- Great _____Exc

VA
Big Ridge
SW - SR83

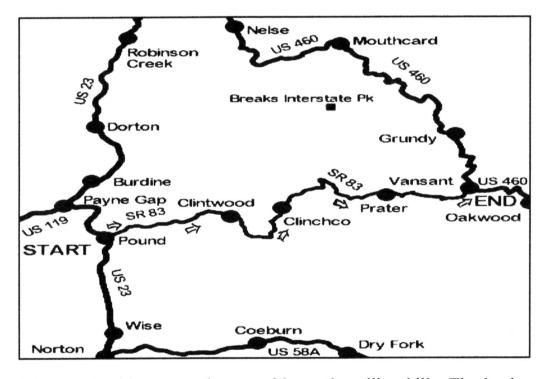

The countryside surrounds you with gently rolling hills. The banks along the McClure River, and Russell Prater Creek provide great rest stop areas. A combination of superb sweepers, and hard banking curves highlight this run. The great road conditions, and wide flowing sweepers give you a smooth ride. I wouldn't get too relaxed, the more challenging corners of this run might surprise you. Oh, what fun we have!

Road Evaluation

ROAD REFERENCE: **R#VA02 - BIG RIDGE**

RUN DISTANCE: 42- Miles

ELEVATION: 1400- Ft > 2200- Ft

SPEED LIMITS: XXX- 15-25mph XXX- 35mph XXX- 45mph _____55mph _____65+mph

RUN EVALUATION: _____Lots Of Fun // A Run To Remember

                           XXX- A Blast To Run // Plenty Of Curves

                           _____Great Run // Major Challenges

                           _____Extreme Ride // Surprises At Every Turn

TYPE OF ROAD: XXX- Sweepers   XXX- Two Lane Traffic

                           XXX- Flowing Curves   _____Four Lane Traffic

                           XXX- Tight Curves   _____Scenic Overlooks / Views

                           _____Extreme Curves   _____National / State Parks

TYPE OF CURVES: XXX- Right Angles _____Uies _____Zs XXX- Ss

POSSIBLE ROAD
HAZARDS: _____Rain Grooves   XXX- Loose Gravel / Sand   _____Pot Holes

                           _____Slick Tar Spots   _____Tunnels   _____Narrow Road

                           _____Bad Banking Curves   _____Un-Even Pavement   _____Animal Xings

                           _____Pedestrians   XXX- Rd Shoulder Drop-Offs _____Blind Curves

                           _____Water Run-Offs   _____Pavement Cracking   XXX- Rock Fall Areas

OVER ALL ROAD
CONDITIONS: _____Ok _____Good XXX- Great _____Exc

VA - KY
Shortt Gap
SW - US460

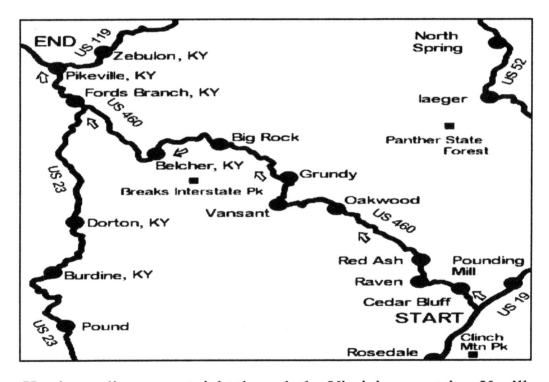

Here's a valley run cut right through the Virginia mountains. You'll start off in Virginia, and make your way to the Kentucky hills. Take a break along the Clinch River, and feel the cool breeze on a hot summer day. The rushing waters of the Levisa Fork River, enhance the pleasures of this ride. Sweepers are the highlight of this run. They are well banked, but don't get too relaxed; something might surprise you.

Road Evaluation

ROAD REFERENCE: **R#VA03 - SHORTT GAP**

RUN DISTANCE: 91- Miles

ELEVATION: 950- Ft > 2850- Ft

SPEED LIMITS: _____15-25mph _____35mph XXX- 45mph XXX- 55mph _____65+mph

RUN EVALUATION: XXX- Lots Of Fun // A Run To Remember

    _____A Blast To Run // Plenty Of Curves

    _____Great Run // Major Challenges

    _____Extreme Ride // Surprises At Every Turn

TYPE OF ROAD:

XXX- Sweepers	_____Two Lane Traffic
XXX- Flowing Curves	XXX- Four Lane Traffic
_____Tight Curves	XXX- Scenic Overlooks / Views
_____Extreme Curves	_____National / State Parks

TYPE OF CURVES: _____Right Angles   XXX- Uies _____Zs   XXX- Ss

POSSIBLE ROAD HAZARDS:

_____Rain Grooves	_____Loose Gravel / Sand	_____Pot Holes
_____Slick Tar Spots	_____Tunnels	_____Narrow Road
_____Bad Banking Curves	_____Un-Even Pavement	_____Animal Xings
_____Pedestrians	_____Rd Shoulder Drop-Offs	_____Blind Curves
XXX- Water Run-Offs	XXX- Pavement Cracking	XXX- Rock Fall Areas

OVER ALL ROAD CONDITIONS: _____Ok _____Good _____Great XXX- Exc

VA
Hanging Rock Valley
SC - SR311/SR159

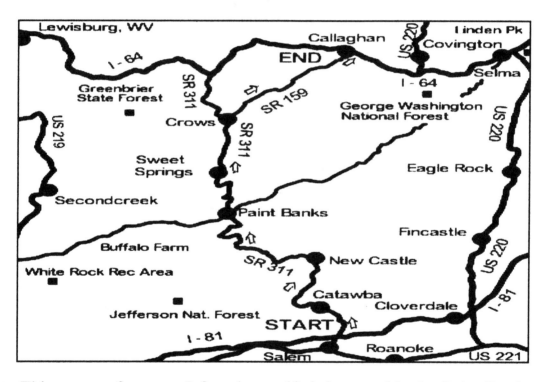

This sunny afternoon, I found myself sitting outside the Paint Bank General Store. A great little place to stop, and talk to the locals. Be sure to get directions to the Buffalo Farm. Your travels will take you through the George Washington, and Jefferson National Forests. This run combines a scenic ride along mountainsides, valleys, and heavily wooded forest roads. A terrific variety of curves will keep you pushing hard.

Road Evaluation

ROAD REFERENCE: **R#VA04 - HANGING ROCK VALLEY**

RUN DISTANCE: 59- Miles

ELEVATION: 1200- Ft > 3500- Ft

SPEED LIMITS: XXX- 15-25mph XXX- 35mph XXX- 45mph XXX- 55mph _____65+mph

RUN EVALUATION:

_____Lots Of Fun // A Run To Remember

_____A Blast To Run // Plenty Of Curves

XXX- Great Run // Major Challenges

_____Extreme Ride // Surprises At Every Turn

TYPE OF ROAD:

XXX- Sweepers	XXX- Two Lane Traffic
XXX- Flowing Curves	_____Four Lane Traffic
XXX- Tight Curves	XXX- Scenic Overlooks / Views
XXX- Extreme Curves	XXX- National / State Parks

TYPE OF CURVES: XXX- Right Angles XXX- Uies XXX- Zs XXX- Ss

POSSIBLE ROAD HAZARDS:

_____Rain Grooves	XXX- Loose Gravel / Sand	_____Pot Holes
_____Slick Tar Spots	XXX- Tunnels	_____Narrow Road
_____Bad Banking Curves	XXX- Un-Even Pavement	_____Animal Xings
_____Pedestrians	XXX- Rd Shoulder Drop-Offs	XXX- Blind Curves
XXX- Water Run-Offs	XXX- Pavement Cracking	XXX- Rock Fall Areas

OVER ALL ROAD CONDITIONS: _____Ok _____Good XXX- Great _____Exc

VA - WV
Monterey Mountain
NC - US250

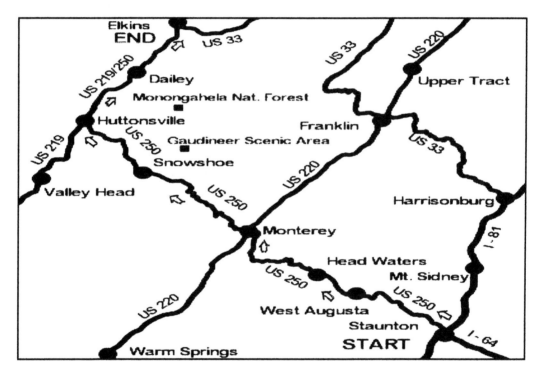

The Monongahela National Forest makes a nice setting for this ride. Wide open valleys, corn fields, rushing rivers, and country farms all add to the warmth of this run. It's hard to beat the panoramic views in this area. They get a four star rating in scenery. The town of Monterey, built in the 1800's, makes a great place to stop. The twisties only add to the pleasures of this run. A must for your travels!!!

Road Evaluation

ROAD REFERENCE: **R#VA05 - MONTEREY MOUNTAIN**

RUN DISTANCE: 86- Miles

ELEVATION: 1350- Ft > 4300- Ft

SPEED LIMITS: XXX- 15-25mph XXX- 35mph XXX- 45mph XXX- 55mph _____65+mph

RUN EVALUATION: _____Lots Of Fun // A Run To Remember

_____A Blast To Run // Plenty Of Curves

XXX- Great Run // Major Challenges

_____Extreme Ride // Surprises At Every Turn

TYPE OF ROAD:

XXX- Sweepers	XXX- Two Lane Traffic
XXX- Flowing Curves	_____Four Lane Traffic
XXX- Tight Curves	XXX- Scenic Overlooks / Views
XXX- Extreme Curves	_____National / State Parks

TYPE OF CURVES: XXX- Right Angles   XXX- Uies   XXX- Zs   XXX- Ss

POSSIBLE ROAD HAZARDS:

_____Rain Grooves	XXX- Loose Gravel / Sand	XXX- Pot Holes
_____Slick Tar Spots	_____Tunnels	_____Narrow Road
XXX- Bad Banking Curves	XXX- Un-Even Pavement	XXX- Animal Xings
_____Pedestrians	XXX- Rd Shoulder Drop-Offs	XXX- Blind Curves
XXX- Water Run-Offs	XXX- Pavement Cracking	XXX- Rock Fall Areas

OVER ALL ROAD CONDITIONS: _____Ok _____Good XXX- Great _____Exc

VA
Hungry Mother
SW - SR16

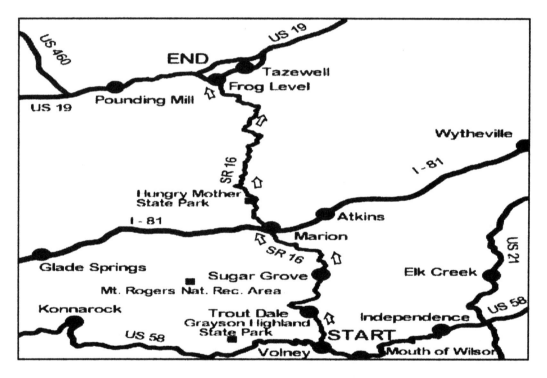

Superb is understating the quality of this run. Traveling through the Jefferson National Forest, you will have the opportunity to enjoy the Mount Rogers National Recreational Area, and the Hungry Mother State Park. The camping and lake areas are some of the best around. Experience the beauty of lush valleys, rolling hills, green pastures, and spectacular views. Oh, and the best of the best in curvessss. Exxxtreme!!!

Road Evaluation

ROAD REFERENCE: **R#VA06 - HUNGRY MOTHER**

RUN DISTANCE: 53- Miles

ELEVATION: 1800- Ft > 3700- Ft

SPEED LIMITS: XXX- 15-25mph XXX- 35mph XXX- 45mph XXX- 55mph _____65+mph

RUN EVALUATION:
_____Lots Of Fun // A Run To Remember

_____A Blast To Run // Plenty Of Curves

_____Great Run // Major Challenges

XXX- Extreme Ride // Surprises At Every Turn

TYPE OF ROAD:

XXX- Sweepers	XXX- Two Lane Traffic
XXX- Flowing Curves	XXX- Four Lane Traffic
XXX- Tight Curves	XXX- Scenic Overlooks / Views
XXX- Extreme Curves	XXX- National / State Parks

TYPE OF CURVES: XXX- Right Angles   XXX- Uies   XXX- Zs   XXX- Ss

POSSIBLE ROAD HAZARDS:

_____Rain Grooves	XXX- Loose Gravel / Sand	_____Pot Holes
_____Slick Tar Spots	_____Tunnels	_____Narrow Road
_____Bad Banking Curves	_____Un-Even Pavement	XXX- Animal Xings
_____Pedestrians	XXX- Rd Shoulder Drop-Offs	XXX- Blind Curves
XXX- Water Run-Offs	XXX- Pavement Cracking	XXX- Rock Fall Areas

OVER ALL ROAD CONDITIONS: _____Ok _____Good XXX- Great _____Exc

VA
Bear Tree Gap
SW - US58

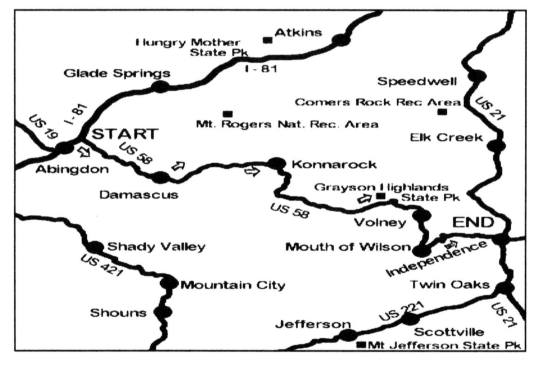

US58 is a combination of the Highland, and Graceson Parkway. Following along the rushing waters of the Holston North Fork River, Beaver Dam Creek, and Big Willow Creek, you can enjoy the heavily wooded Mount Rogers National Forest. The Gracesons Highland State Park, and Virginia Creeper Trail are great pull-overs for hikes, or picnics. The exxtreme curves will keep you on the edge. Stay alert!

Road Evaluation

ROAD REFERENCE: R#VA07 - BEAR TREE GAP

RUN DISTANCE: 61- Miles

ELEVATION: 1800- Ft > 4000- Ft

SPEED LIMITS: XXX- 15-25mph XXX- 35mph XXX- 45mph XXX- 55mph _____65+mph

RUN EVALUATION: _____Lots Of Fun

_____A Blast To Run

XXX- Great Run // Major Challenges

_____ Extreme Ride // Surprises At Every Turn

TYPE OF ROAD:

XXX- Sweepers	XXX- Two Lane Traffic
XXX- Flowing Curves	_____Four Lane Traffic
XXX- Tight Curves	XXX- Scenic Overlooks / Views
XXX- Extreme Curves	XXX- National / State Parks

TYPE OF CURVES: XXX- Right Angles XXX- Uies XXX- Zs XXX- Ss

POSSIBLE ROAD HAZARDS:

_____Rain Grooves	XXX- Loose Gravel / Sand	_____Pot Holes
_____Slick Tar Spots	_____Tunnels	_____Narrow Road
_____Bad Banking Curves	_____Un-Even Pavement	XXX- Animal Xings
XXX- Pedestrians	XXX- Rd Shoulder Drop-Offs	XXX- Blind Curves
_____Water Run-Offs	XXX- Pavement Cracking	XXX- Rock Fall Areas

OVER ALL ROAD CONDITIONS: _____Ok _____Good XXX- Great _____Exc

VA
Rocky Knob
SC - US221/SR8/SR40

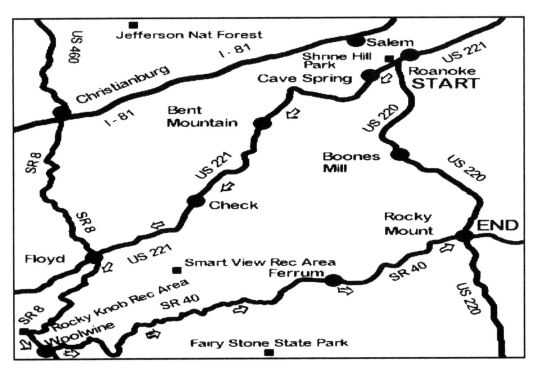

Now here is the run that will challenge, and excite everyone. This area is beautifully wooded with trees draping the roadway. The countryside is dotted with apple orchards, and Christmas tree farms. You will be especially rewarded by the mountain, and valley views. The combination of these roads, will offer everything from serious sweepers to some very extreme "S" cornering curves. Taste the fruit!

Road Evaluation

ROAD REFERENCE: **R#VA08 - ROCKY KNOB**

RUN DISTANCE: 109- Miles

ELEVATION: 1150- Ft > 3100- Ft

SPEED LIMITS: XXX- 15-25mph XXX- 35mph XXX- 45mph XXX- 55mph _____65+mph

RUN EVALUATION:

    _____Lots Of Fun // A Run To Remember

    _____A Blast To Run // Plenty Of Curves

    _____Great Run // Major Challenges

    XXX- Extreme Ride // Surprises At Every Turn

TYPE OF ROAD:

XXX- Sweepers	XXX- Two Lane Traffic
XXX- Flowing Curves	_____Four Lane Traffic
XXX- Tight Curves	XXX- Scenic Overlooks / Views
XXX- Extreme Curves	_____National / State Parks

TYPE OF CURVES: XXX- Right Angles XXX- Uies XXX- Zs XXX- Ss

POSSIBLE ROAD HAZARDS:

_____Rain Grooves	XXX- Loose Gravel / Sand	XXX- Pot Holes
_____Slick Tar Spots	_____Tunnels	XXX- Narrow Road
_____Bad Banking Curves	_____Un-Even Pavement	XXX- Animal Xings
_____Pedestrians	XXX- Rd Shoulder Drop-Offs	XXX- Blind Curves
XXX- Water Run-Offs	XXX- Pavement Cracking	XXX- Rock Fall Areas

OVER ALL ROAD CONDITIONS: _____Ok _____Good XXX- Great _____Exc

VA - WV
Big Turn
NC - SR39

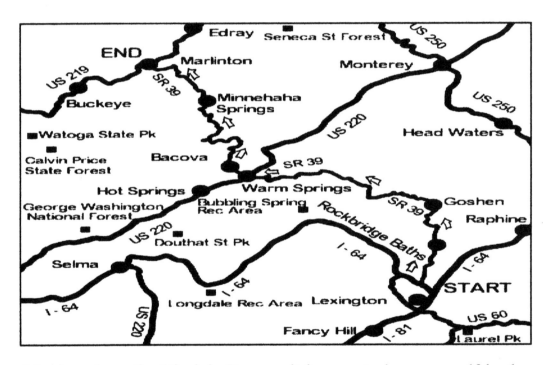

Moving along the Virginia Byway, it is easy to lose yourself in the beautiful valley views, bordering mountains, and winding roads. Terrific "S" cornering highlights this run! I found the traffic very light, travelling through the George Washington National Forest, and Watoga State Park. There are several great spots for a picnic. The historical town of Huntersville, WV, was a nice place to break for lunch.

Road Evaluation

ROAD REFERENCE: R#VA09 - BIG TURN

RUN DISTANCE: 72- Miles

ELEVATION: 1000- Ft > 2850- Ft

SPEED LIMITS: XXX- 15-25mph XXX- 35mph XXX- 45mph XXX- 55mph _____65+mph

RUN EVALUATION: _____Lots Of Fun // A Run To Remember

        _____A Blast To Run // Plenty Of Curves

        XXX- Great Run // Major Challenges

        _____Extreme Ride // Surprises At Every Turn

TYPE OF ROAD:

XXX- Sweepers	XXX- Two Lane Traffic
XXX- Flowing Curves	_____Four Lane Traffic
XXX- Tight Curves	XXX- Scenic Overlooks / Views
XXX- Extreme Curves	XXX- National / State Parks

TYPE OF CURVES: XXX- Right Angles   XXX- Uies   _____Zs   XXX- Ss

POSSIBLE ROAD HAZARDS:

_____Rain Grooves	XXX- Loose Gravel / Sand	_____Pot Holes
_____Slick Tar Spots	_____Tunnels	_____Narrow Road
_____Bad Banking Curves	_____Un-Even Pavement	XXX- Animal Xings
_____Pedestrians	XXX- Rd Shoulder Drop-Offs	XXX- Blind Curves
XXX- Water Run-Offs	_____Pavement Cracking	XXX- Rock Fall Areas

OVER ALL ROAD CONDITIONS: _____Ok _____Good XXX- Great _____Exc

WEST VIRGINIA
Twisties

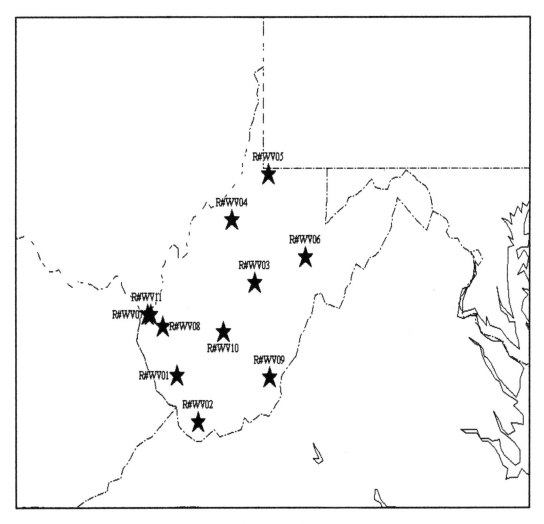

WEST VIRGINIA RUN LIST

REFERENCE GUIDE
RUN SHEET
State ID
Run Name
State Map Location - Road ID
STATE MAP
Star Shows Run# (R#) Location

WV
Twilight Loop
SW - SR17/SR85

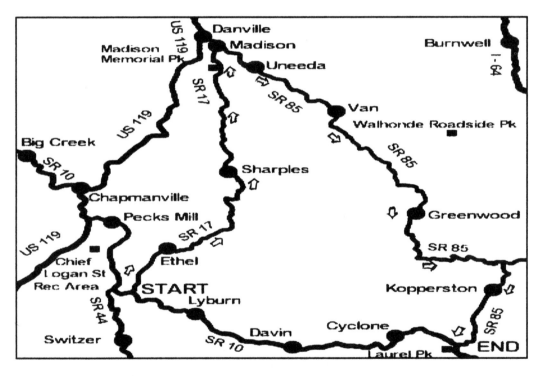

This scenic valley run is chocked full of great river spots to pull off the road. The quaintness of country life is seen in many areas along the river. Suspension bridges across the river dot the countryside. The old timey one lane bridges add that special touch, and sometimes a thrill or two when traffic meets. An excellent series of right angle curves, and "U" corners will make for an exciting days ride.

Road Evaluation

ROAD REFERENCE: R#WV01 - TWILIGHT LOOP

RUN DISTANCE: 73- Miles

ELEVATION: 800- Ft > 2900- Ft

SPEED LIMITS: XXX- 15-25mph   XXX- 35mph   XXX- 45mph   XXX- 55mph   _____65+mph

RUN EVALUATION:

_____Lots Of Fun // A Run To Remember

_____A Blast To Run // Plenty Of Curves

XXX- Great Run // Major Challenges

_____Extreme Ride // Surprises At Every Turn

TYPE OF ROAD:

XXX- Sweepers	XXX- Two Lane Traffic
XXX- Flowing Curves	_____Four Lane Traffic
XXX- Tight Curves	XXX- Scenic Overlooks / Views
XXX- Extreme Curves	_____National / State Parks

TYPE OF CURVES: XXX- Right Angles   XXX- Uies _____Zs   XXX- Ss

POSSIBLE ROAD HAZARDS:

_____Rain Grooves	XXX- Loose Gravel / Sand	_____Pot Holes
_____Slick Tar Spots	_____Tunnels	XXX- Narrow Road
_____Bad Banking Curves	XXX- Un-Even Pavement	_____Animal Xings
XXX- Pedestrians	XXX- Rd Shoulder Drop-Offs	XXX- Blind Curves
XXX- Water Run-Offs	XXX- Pavement Cracking	XXX- Rock Fall Areas

OVER ALL ROAD CONDITIONS: _____Ok _____Good   XXX- Great _____Exc

WV
Deadman Hollow Loop
SC - SR16/SR161/SR103

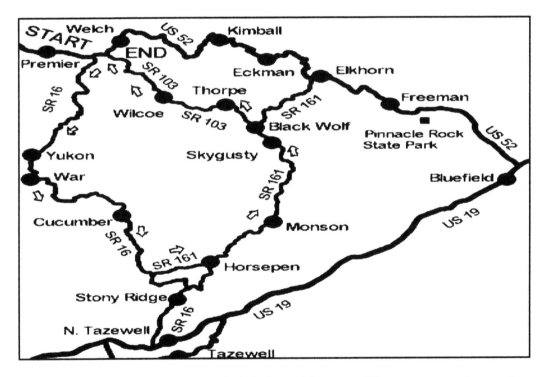

Dip and Twist cornering highlights this run. The curves along the ridge are only half the fun these roads offer you. Fast "S" curves along the Tug Fork River, will make the day even better. Picturesque valleys, slow moving creeks, and lush forest areas add that special magic found on great runs. Around the coal mining areas the roads have signs, "Slippery when wet". Heed the warnings, and have a safe ride.

Road Evaluation

ROAD REFERENCE: R#WV02 - DEADMAN HOLLOW LOOP

RUN DISTANCE: 52- Miles

ELEVATION: 1400- Ft > 2700- Ft

SPEED LIMITS: XXX- 15-25mph XXX- 35mph XXX- 45mph XXX- 55mph _____65+mph

RUN EVALUATION: _____Lots Of Fun // A Run To Remember

_____A Blast To Run // Plenty Of Curves

XXX- Great Run // Major Challenges

_____Extreme Ride // Surprises At Every Turn

TYPE OF ROAD:

XXX- Sweepers	XXX- Two Lane Traffic
XXX- Flowing Curves	_____Four Lane Traffic
XXX- Tight Curves	_____Scenic Overlooks / Views
XXX- Extreme Curves	_____National / State Parks

TYPE OF CURVES: XXX- Right Angles XXX- Uies XXX- Zs XXX- Ss

POSSIBLE ROAD HAZARDS:

_____Rain Grooves	XXX- Loose Gravel / Sand	_____Pot Holes
XXX- Slick Tar Spots	_____Tunnels	XXX- Narrow Road
_____Bad Banking Curves	XXX- Un-Even Pavement	_____Animal Xings
XXX- Pedestrians	XXX- Rd Shoulder Drop-Offs	_____Blind Curves
_____Water Run-Offs	XXX- Pavement Cracking	XXX- Rock Fall Areas

OVER ALL ROAD CONDITIONS: _____Ok _____Good XXX- Great _____Exc

WV
Big Run
CC - SR15

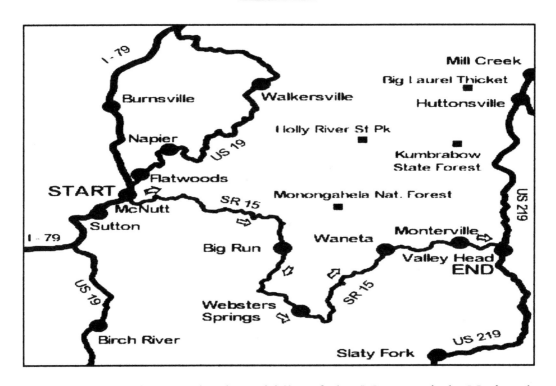

Adventure awaits you in the middle of the Monongahela National Forest. There you will find a beautiful river winding along a curvy little road. The umbrella effect of trees shading the road, and the sound of rushing water add special warmth to this natural setting. You'll have a wide variety of continuous curves, as you ride through dense woods, open pastureland, & steep mountain ridges. Great sweepers!!!

Road Evaluation

ROAD REFERENCE: R#WV03 - BIG RUN

RUN DISTANCE: 66- Miles

ELEVATION: 900- Ft > 3525- Ft

SPEED LIMITS: XXX- 15-25mph XXX- 35mph XXX- 45mph XXX- 55mph _____65+mph

RUN EVALUATION: _____Lots Of Fun // A Run To Remember

XXX- A Blast To Run // Plenty Of Curves

_____Great Run // Major Challenges

_____Extreme Ride // Surprises At Every Turn

TYPE OF ROAD:

XXX- Sweepers	XXX- Two Lane Traffic
XXX- Flowing Curves	_____Four Lane Traffic
XXX- Tight Curves	XXX- Scenic Overlooks / Views
_____Extreme Curves	XXX- National / State Parks

TYPE OF CURVES: XXX- Right Angles _____Uies _____Zs XXX- Ss

POSSIBLE ROAD HAZARDS:

_____Rain Grooves	XXX- Loose Gravel / Sand	XXX- Pot Holes
_____Slick Tar Spots	_____Tunnels	XXX- Narrow Road
_____Bad Banking Curves	_____Un-Even Pavement	_____Animal Xings
_____Pedestrians	XXX- Rd Shoulder Drop-Offs	XXX- Blind Curves
XXX- Water Run-Offs	XXX- Pavement Cracking	XXX- Rock Fall Areas

OVER ALL ROAD CONDITIONS: _____Ok _____Good XXX- Great _____Exc

WV
Standingrock
NW - SR16

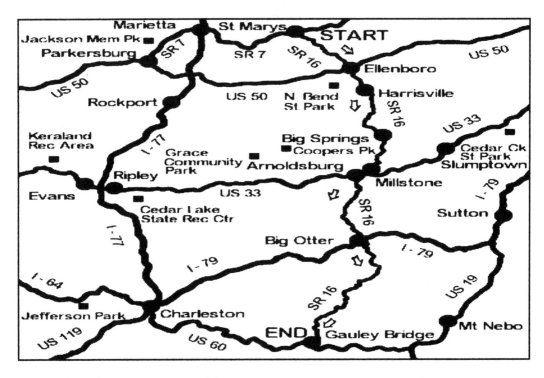

One of the very best! That's one way to describe this run. Intense curves from start to finish will send you dancing along the mountain ridges. Moving down in the valley, you will enjoy the view of rolling hills surrounding the fenced pastures. The area has much to discover from times of yesterday. Historical towns from the 1800's reveal a look into our past. For another beautiful stop, try the North Bend State Park.

Road Evaluation

ROAD REFERENCE: **R#WV04 - STANDINGROCK**

RUN DISTANCE: 96- Miles

ELEVATION: 700- Ft > 1500- Ft

SPEED LIMITS: XXX- 15-25mph XXX- 35mph XXX- 45mph XXX- 55mph _____65+mph

RUN EVALUATION:

    _____Lots Of Fun // A Run To Remember

    _____A Blast To Run // Plenty Of Curves

    _____Great Run // Major Challenges

    XXX- Extreme Ride // Surprises At Every Turn

TYPE OF ROAD:

_____Sweepers	XXX- Two Lane Traffic
XXX- Flowing Curves	_____Four Lane Traffic
XXX- Tight Curves	XXX- Scenic Overlooks / Views
XXX- Extreme Curves	XXX- National / State Parks

TYPE OF CURVES: XXX- Right Angles   XXX- Uies   XXX- Zs   XXX- Ss

POSSIBLE ROAD HAZARDS:

_____Rain Grooves	XXX- Loose Gravel / Sand	XXX- Pot Holes
_____Slick Tar Spots	_____Tunnels	XXX- Narrow Road
_____Bad Banking Curves	XXX- Un-Even Pavement	XXX- Animal Xings
XXX- Pedestrians	XXX- Rd Shoulder Drop-Offs	XXX- Blind Curves
_____Water Run-Offs	XXX- Pavement Cracking	XXX- Rock Fall Areas

OVER ALL ROAD CONDITIONS: _____Ok _____Good XXX- Great _____Exc

WV
Porters Fall
NC - SR7/SR20

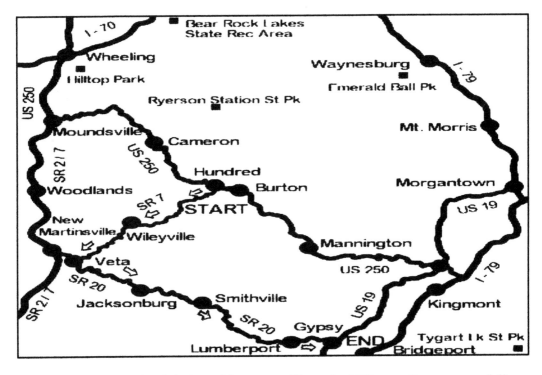

Oh, what a wonderful day this run will make! Horse farms, sparkling creeks, open fields, and an excellent series of well banked sweepers. These high speed sweepers are made even better when combined with the fantastic dip and twist curves on SR7. You'll see terrific views from the ridges, and pass by several interesting spots along the way. A place that will catch your eye, is an 1840s white frame Baptist Church.

Road Evaluation

ROAD REFERENCE: **R#WV05 - PORTERS FALL**

RUN DISTANCE: 73- Miles

ELEVATION: 790- Ft > 1385- Ft

SPEED LIMITS: XXX- 15-25mph XXX- 35mph XXX- 45mph XXX- 55mph _____65+mph

RUN EVALUATION: _____Lots Of Fun // A Run To Remember

_____A Blast To Run // Plenty Of Curves

XXX- Great Run // Major Challenges

_____Extreme Ride // Surprises At Every Turn

TYPE OF ROAD:

XXX- Sweepers   XXX- Two Lane Traffic

XXX- Flowing Curves   _____Four Lane Traffic

XXX- Tight Curves   XXX- Scenic Overlooks / Views

XXX- Extreme Curves   _____National / State Parks

TYPE OF CURVES: XXX- Right Angles   XXX- Uies   XXX- Zs   XXX- Ss

POSSIBLE ROAD HAZARDS:

_____Rain Grooves	XXX- Loose Gravel / Sand	XXX- Pot Holes
_____Slick Tar Spots	_____Tunnels	_____Narrow Road
_____Bad Banking Curves	XXX- Un-Even Pavement	XXX- Animal Xings
XXX- Pedestrians	XXX- Rd Shoulder Drop-Offs	XXX- Blind Curves
XXX- Water Run-Offs	XXX- Pavement Cracking	XXX- Rock Fall Areas

OVER ALL ROAD CONDITIONS: _____Ok _____Good XXX- Great _____Exc

WV - VA
Senoca Rock
NE - US33

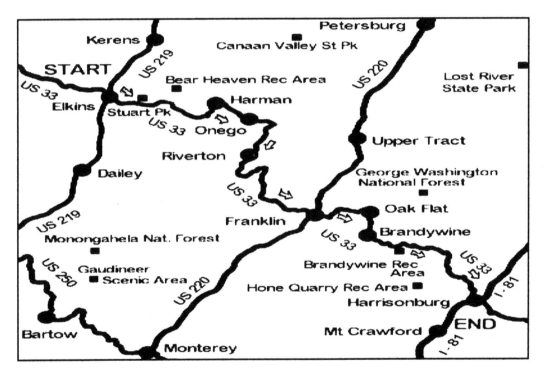

Speeding through the George Washington National Forest was quite nice this chilly morning. The mountains had seen their first snow, but the roads were clear. Some serious cornering on the mountain ridges, highlighted by several sets of fast moving "S" curves, guarantees you an exciting ride. From the mountain tops, you can see fantastic panoramic views. Senoca Rocks offers an unusual, and unique site. Giant rocks!

Road Evaluation

ROAD REFERENCE: **R#WV06 - SENOCA ROCK**

RUN DISTANCE: 100- Miles

ELEVATION: 1475- Ft > 3600- Ft

SPEED LIMITS: XXX- 15-25mph   XXX- 35mph   XXX- 45mph   XXX- 55mph   _____65+mph

RUN EVALUATION: _____Lots Of Fun

                               _____A Blast To Run

                               XXX- Great Run // Major Challenges

                               _____Extreme Ride // Surprises At Every Turn

TYPE OF ROAD: XXX- Sweepers   XXX- Two Lane Traffic

                               XXX- Flowing Curves   XXX- Four Lane Traffic

                               XXX- Tight Curves   XXX- Scenic Overlooks / Views

                               XXX- Extreme Curves   XXX- National / State Parks

TYPE OF CURVES: XXX- Right Angles   XXX- Uies   XXX- Zs   XXX- Ss

POSSIBLE ROAD HAZARDS:

_____Rain Grooves	XXX- Loose Gravel / Sand	_____Pot Holes
XXX- Slick Tar Spots	_____Tunnels	_____Narrow Road
_____Bad Banking Curves	XXX- Un-Even Pavement	_____Animal Xings
XXX- Pedestrians	XXX- Rd Shoulder Drop-Offs	XXX- Blind Curves
XXX- Water Run-Offs	XXX- Pavement Cracking	XXX- Rock Fall Areas

OVER ALL ROAD CONDITIONS: _____Ok   _____Good   XXX- Great _____Exc

WV
Guyandotte River
SW - SR10

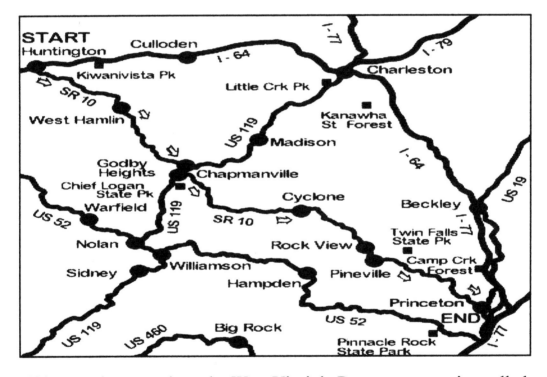

This run takes you along the West Virginia Byway on a section called the Coal Heritage Trail. The countryside is quite scenic with small farms dotting the winding roads. Much of the area is heavily wooded, umbrellaing the road. The Beech Fork and Chief Logan State Parks provide excellent areas to pass the afternoon, or stop overnight. Enjoy the variety of curves, from easy to extreme. A thrill for anyone!

Road Evaluation

ROAD REFERENCE: R#WV07 - GUYANDOTTE RIVER

RUN DISTANCE: 149- Miles

ELEVATION: 600- Ft > 3000- Ft

SPEED LIMITS: XXX- 15-25mph XXX- 35mph XXX- 45mph XXX- 55mph _____65+mph

RUN EVALUATION:
_____Lots Of Fun // A Run To Remember

XXX- A Blast To Run // Plenty Of Curves

_____Great Run // Major Challenges

_____Extreme Ride // Surprises At Every Turn

TYPE OF ROAD:

XXX- Sweepers	XXX- Two Lane Traffic
XXX- Flowing Curves	_____Four Lane Traffic
XXX- Tight Curves	_____Scenic Overlooks / Views
XXX- Extreme Curves	XXX- National / State Parks

TYPE OF CURVES: XXX- Right Angles   XXX- Uies   _____Zs   XXX- Ss

POSSIBLE ROAD HAZARDS:

_____Rain Grooves	XXX- Loose Gravel / Sand	XXX- Pot Holes
_____Slick Tar Spots	_____Tunnels	_____Narrow Road
_____Bad Banking Curves	_____Un-Even Pavement	_____Animal Xings
_____Pedestrians	XXX- Rd Shoulder Drop-Offs	XXX- Blind Curves
XXX- Water Run-Offs	XXX- Pavement Cracking	XXX- Rock Fall Areas

OVER ALL ROAD CONDITIONS: _____Ok _____Good XXX- Great _____Exc

WV
Marsh Fork
SW - SR3

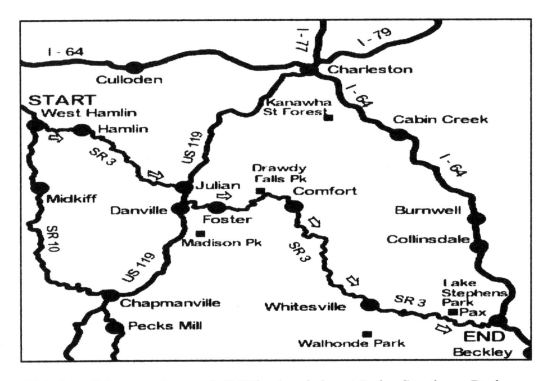

This is a fisherman's special! Whether it be at Lake Stephens Park, or trout fishing on the Coal River, you will have quite a day. Now add the valley overlooks, and beautiful Cypress trees, combined with an artistic view of the mountains, and you have the makings of a very special day. Fast sweeping curves added to some serious dip and twist cornering perfects this backroad experience. The coal trains slowly pass by.

Road Evaluation

ROAD REFERENCE: R#WV08 - MARSH FORK

RUN DISTANCE: 65- Miles

ELEVATION: 650- Ft > 2500- Ft

SPEED LIMITS: XXX- 15-25mph   XXX- 35mph   XXX- 45mph   XXX- 55mph   65+mph

RUN EVALUATION: _____Lots Of Fun // A Run To Remember

XXX- A Blast To Run // Plenty Of Curves

_____Great Run // Major Challenges

_____Extreme Ride // Surprises At Every Turn

TYPE OF ROAD:

XXX- Sweepers	XXX- Two Lane Traffic
XXX- Flowing Curves	_____Four Lane Traffic
XXX- Tight Curves	XXX- Scenic Overlooks / Views
_____Extreme Curves	_____National / State Parks

TYPE OF CURVES: XXX- Right Angles   XXX- Uies   _____Zs   XXX- Ss

POSSIBLE ROAD HAZARDS:

_____Rain Grooves	_____Loose Gravel / Sand	XXX- Pot Holes
XXX- Slick Tar Spots	_____Tunnels	_____Narrow Road
_____Bad Banking Curves	XXX- Un-Even Pavement	XXX- Animal Xings
XXX- Pedestrians	XXX- Rd Shoulder Drop-Offs	_____Blind Curves
XXX- Water Run-Offs	XXX- Pavement Cracking	XXX- Rock Fall Areas

OVER ALL ROAD CONDITIONS: _____Ok _____Good   XXX- Great _____Exc

WV
Tygart Valley River
SE - US219/US50

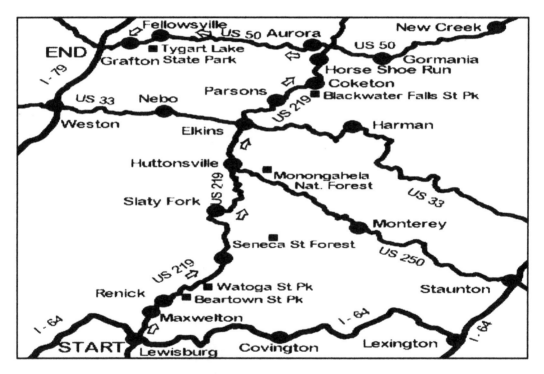

There is very little this run leaves out. Some interesting sites include 1800's farmhouses, churches, and historical towns. The scenic countryside surrounds you with fields of wildflowers, breathtaking panoramic valley views, and amazing lineations of distant mountains. Take a break at one of the many State Parks. Great "S" cornering, and very little traffic make for a fun road trip. Ezzz riding!

Road Evaluation

ROAD REFERENCE: **R#WV09 - TAGART VALLEY RIVER**

RUN DISTANCE: 149- Miles

ELEVATION: 975- Ft > 3650- Ft

SPEED LIMITS: XXX- 15-25mph XXX- 35mph XXX- 45mph XXX- 55mph _____65+mph

RUN EVALUATION: _____Lots Of Fun // A Run To Remember

_____A Blast To Run // Plenty Of Curves

XXX- Great Run // Major Challenges

_____Extreme Ride // Surprises At Every Turn

TYPE OF ROAD:

XXX- Sweepers	XXX- Two Lane Traffic
XXX- Flowing Curves	_____Four Lane Traffic
XXX- Tight Curves	XXX- Scenic Overlooks / Views
XXX- Extreme Curves	XXX- National / State Parks

TYPE OF CURVES: XXX- Right Angles   XXX- Uies   XXX- Zs   XXX- Ss

POSSIBLE ROAD HAZARDS:

_____Rain Grooves	XXX- Loose Gravel / Sand	_____Pot Holes
_____Slick Tar Spots	_____Tunnels	_____Narrow Road
_____Bad Banking Curves	_____Un-Even Pavement	XXX- Animal Xings
_____Pedestrians	_____Rd Shoulder Drop-Offs	XXX- Blind Curves
_____Water Run-Offs	XXX- Pavement Cracking	_____Rock Fall Areas

OVER ALL ROAD CONDITIONS: _____Ok _____Good XXX- Great _____Exc

WV
Highland's Scenic Byway
SC - SR39

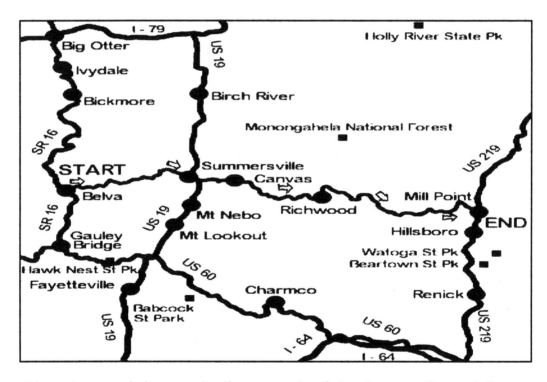

There I was, sitting on the front porch of the Canvas General Store, sipping a coke, and reflecting on the last thirty miles. Plenty of fast moving curves, and loose sweepers winding through the heavily wooded Monongahela National Forest. This run will be a favorite if old 1800's churches interest you. The area is quite beautiful with clusters of Cypress trees, shady backroads, lush rolling pastures, and rippling falls.

Road Evaluation

ROAD REFERENCE: R#WV10 - HIGHLANDS SCENIC BYWAY

RUN DISTANCE: 89- Miles

ELEVATION: 800- Ft > 3900- Ft

SPEED LIMITS: XXX- 15-25mph XXX- 35mph XXX- 45mph XXX- 55mph _____65+mph

RUN EVALUATION: _____Lots Of Fun // A Run To Remember

_____A Blast To Run // Plenty Of Curves

XXX- Great Run // Major Challenges

_____Extreme Ride // Surprises At Every Turn

TYPE OF ROAD:

XXX- Sweepers	XXX- Two Lane Traffic
XXX- Flowing Curves	_____Four Lane Traffic
XXX- Tight Curves	XXX- Scenic Overlooks / Views
XXX- Extreme Curves	XXX- National / State Parks

TYPE OF CURVES: XXX- Right Angles   XXX- Uies   _____Zs   XXX- Ss

POSSIBLE ROAD HAZARDS:

_____Rain Grooves	XXX- Loose Gravel / Sand	XXX- Pot Holes
XXX- Slick Tar Spots	_____Tunnels	_____Narrow Road
_____Bad Banking Curves	XXX- Un-Even Pavement	_____Animal Xings
XXX- Pedestrians	XXX- Rd Shoulder Drop-Offs	XXX- Blind Curves
XXX- Water Run-Offs	XXX- Pavement Cracking	XXX- Rock Fall Areas

OVER ALL ROAD CONDITIONS: _____Ok _____Good XXX- Great _____Exc

WV
Twelvepole Creek
SW - SR152/US52/SR65/SR97

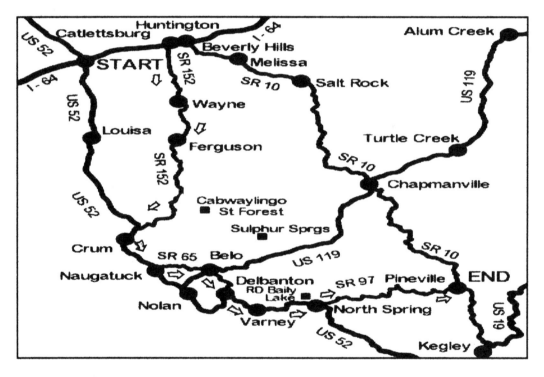

Welcome to the West Virginia Byway. Throughout the coal mining country, you will discover beautiful valleys, thick forest areas, and the quaint communities dotting the countryside. Coal trains lead the way to several fine backroad adventures. Pinnacle State Park makes a wonderful afternoon stop, and don't forget to check out the R.D. Bailey Lake resort area. Curves get tricky, so brake a little.

Road Evaluation

ROAD REFERENCE: R#WV11 - TWELVEPOLE CREEK

RUN DISTANCE: 134- Miles

ELEVATION: 550- Ft > 1050- Ft

SPEED LIMITS: XXX- 15-25mph XXX- 35mph XXX- 45mph XXX- 55mph XXX- 65+mph

RUN EVALUATION:

_____Lots Of Fun // A Run To Remember

_____A Blast To Run // Plenty Of Curves

XXX- Great Run // Major Challenges

_____Extreme Ride // Surprises At Every Turn

TYPE OF ROAD:

XXX- Sweepers	XXX- Two Lane Traffic
XXX- Flowing Curves	XXX- Four Lane Traffic
XXX- Tight Curves	XXX- Scenic Overlooks / Views
_____Extreme Curves	XXX- National / State Parks

TYPE OF CURVES: XXX- Right Angles XXX- Uies XXX- Zs XXX- Ss

POSSIBLE ROAD HAZARDS:

_____Rain Grooves	XXX- Loose Gravel / Sand	XXX- Pot Holes
_____Slick Tar Spots	_____Tunnels	_____Narrow Road
_____Bad Banking Curves	XXX- Un-Even Pavement	XXX- Animal Xings
XXX- Pedestrians	XXX- Rd Shoulder Drop-Offs	XXX- Blind Curves
_____Water Run-Offs	XXX- Pavement Cracking	XXX- Rock Fall Areas

OVER ALL ROAD CONDITIONS: _____Ok _____Good XXX- Great _____Exc

Notes

Notes

Notes